# estherpress

## Books for Courageous Women

### ESTHER PRESS VISION

*Publishing diverse voices that encourage and equip women to walk courageously in the light of God's truth for such a time as this.*

### BIBLICAL STATEMENT OF PURPOSE

*"For if you remain silent at this time, relief and deliverance for the Jews will arise from another place, but you and your father's family will perish. And who knows but that you have come to your royal position for such a time as this?"*

– Esther 4:14

What people are saying about ...

# ENTRUSTED TO LEAD

"This is the book I wish I had when I started my leadership journey. In *Entrusted to Lead*, Donna provides a framework to understand the unique challenges women navigate in order to step into their calling and leadership potential and offers pathways to move forward. Honest. Vulnerable. Inspiring. Empowering."

**Christine Caine**, founder of
A21 and Propel Women

"Donna Pisani's passionate devotion to God and His Word permeates every facet of who she is as a wife, mom, grandmother, friend, and spiritual leader. She embodies the kind of wise humility that reflects a very long walk of obedience. When it comes to authority, there's a profound difference between those who are entrusted and those who are entitled, and Donna is firmly planted in the first camp. The many decades of integrity and biblical fidelity demonstrated in her personal life and public ministry reveal that she is divinely entrusted and is therefore a trustworthy guide to help Christ followers navigate the doctrinal nuances of the mighty throng of women (Psalm 68:11) our Creator Redeemer has raised/is raising up for His kingdom purposes."

**Lisa Harper**, speaker, Bible teacher
and author of *Life* and *Jesus*

"This book is a profound gift delivered at the perfect moment in time. Donna's love for the Word of God and for women called to a place of influence and leadership in the church soaks every page. If you find yourself a little weary on your journey or longing for support and an encouraging voice, you have found the perfect traveling companion."

**Sheila Walsh**, author and TV host

"In *Entrusted to Lead*, Donna unpacks her decades of experience leading and her infectious love of leadership to encourage leaders to rise up into the fullness of the God-given influence God has gifted them to steward. Leadership is something entrusted to us by Jesus, not something we're entitled to—and none of us want to be leaders who do more leading than following Jesus. Donna cuts through the internal lies that prevent leaders from pursuing their calling and unpacks the purpose and potential of being an incredible leader. Not by frantically leading more, but by obediently following Jesus."

**Shelley Giglio**, chief strategist, director of Label
Operations and Artist Management for sixstepsrecords
and co-founder of the Passion Movement

"In *Entrusted to Lead*, Dr. Donna Pisani offers practical advice and a deeply rooted biblical perspective on women in leadership. This book gives you the tools to confront the internal doubts and lies that often hold us back from fully embracing what God has entrusted to us. Whether you're wrestling with God's call to leadership or feeling isolated in your journey, this book extends guidance and encouragement every step of the way. Donna reminds us that, as women, we have a stunning role in God's kingdom, and we are called to lead with boldness and grace. *Entrusted to Lead* is not just a book; it's a manifesto for women ready to rise up, step into their God-given purpose, and live the flourishing life He calls them to live."

**Jennie Lusko**, pastor of Fresh Life Church
with her husband Levi and bestselling
author of *The Fight to Flourish*

"I love Donna's scholarship, passion, and commitment to help women walk in the calling that God has for them. We need her voice, and I'm grateful that she is taking the time to add to the conversation on women in ministry. She has modeled it well, and I highly recommend that you read her book."

**Greg Surratt**, founding pastor of Seacoast
Church and author of *Ir-rev-rend*

"I wish I had this book when I started my journey as a 21-year-old woman in ministry. It would have helped me with feeling understood and not alone. Donna sheds light on the theology of women in ministry from a biblical perspective and gives her life experiences from what she has learned over several decades. That in itself is pure gold. She writes with eloquence and revelation and shows us what God has always intended for women in leadership. This book is so necessary and will give everyone who reads it tools to lead well with what has been entrusted to them."

**Alex Seeley**, lead pastor of The Belonging Co

"*Entrusted to Lead* is like an experienced and wise guide in the holy world of our Bible, taking you from your world of entitlement into the Jesus-created and Spirit-shaped world of giftedness and entrustedness. Donna will guide you into Scripture for new insights, into your heart for deeper self-awareness, into leadership circles to learn the art of leading, and into the church to learn that God gifts women to do what God gifts them to do. Be Tov!"

**Scot McKnight**,
PhD, professor of New Testament

"Pisani draws on decades of pastoral leadership as she explores women's callings in ministry. *Entrusted to Lead* is grounded on solid biblical foundations and provides a thorough exploration of biblical passages. Pisani focuses on encouragement and community, not conflict, as she considers the perils of entitled leadership. Her robust vision of entrusted leadership that promotes Spirit-led, Christ-centered service for the church and the world will inspire readers to take up their calling with new vigor and joy."

**Lynn H. Cohick**, PhD,
professor of New Testament

"My friend Donna Pisani has written a spectacular book! *Entrusted to Lead* is a transformative guide that illuminates the path to impactful, God-inspired leadership. Through vivid and often hilarious storytelling, as well as practical and inspirational strategies, this book will ignite your passion for leading with purpose. Whether you're a seasoned leader or aspiring to be one, this book is a must-read for anyone who wants to understand the heart behind effective leadership and make a difference in the world."

**Holly Wagner**, founder of Oasis Church and
She Rises and author of *Find Your Brave*

"We can't think of anyone more equipped and anointed to deliver this message than (Dr.) Donna Pisani. *Entrusted to Lead* is an invitation to a leadership lifestyle that champions the gifting and strengths of BOTH men and women and elevates a posture of humility over position or title. It carries the message of the power that is released when the church activates the "full dose" of Hope that is available when sons AND daughters courageously echo God's voice to a desperate world. If you are a woman who has ever questioned your calling to lead, this book will be an infusion of confidence and an impartation of hard-earned wisdom from forty years of living this #sameteam message."

**Todd and Julie Mullins**, senior pastors
of Christ Fellowship Church

"Forget the corner office and the power suit. This book flips the script on leadership, showing it's not about titles or authority, but about responsibility and trust. Donna Pisani weaves her own experiences into a powerful message that will resonate with and resource anyone who is summoned to the front of the lines."

**Leonard Sweet**, author, professor, preacher,
publisher, proprietor of Sanctuary Seaside,
and founder of preachthestory.com

"This book is a gift to the leadership conversation. Donna brings a humble approach balanced with theological grounding and practical experience. Her personal story is incredibly engaging and will challenge women and men alike to believe for greater things in their own lives and callings. This work will give permission and courage for a generation of women and men to lead together on the same team."

**Daniel Floyd**, senior pastor of Lifepoint Church and author of *Living the Dream*

"*Entrusted to Lead* is a refreshing take on leadership that feels like a conversation with a wise and trusted friend. Donna Pisani's biblical insights, personal reflections, and heartfelt wisdom make this book a treasure for anyone seeking to lead with clarity and authority. Whether you're stepping into leadership for the first time or you're a seasoned leader aiming to deepen your impact, this book is precisely what you need. *Entrusted to Lead* is an invitation to embrace your gifts, step into your unique calling, and influence the world with grace and confidence."

**Dr. Terry and Judith Crist**, author of *Loving Samaritans* and co-lead pastors of City of Grace

"To say that we have been anxiously anticipating this book is an understatement. Donna Pisani does a phenomenal and comprehensive job of unpacking a subject that is vitally important to the capital 'C' church. With inspiration and sound theology, she gives practical insight into how women can steward their God-given influence, have a divine contribution, and live out their purpose in a world often resistant to their voice. This book is a much-needed conversation."

**Dr. Jeremy and Rev. Jennifer DeWeerdt**,
senior pastors of City First Church

"Leadership is often portrayed as a solitary role, but it doesn't have to be. The journey the two of us have been on for the last several years has been one of learning how to lead alongside one another, and that is a big part of what this book is about. We love Donna and are so excited for others to learn about what it means to lead together on the #sameteam."

**Josh and Lisa Surratt**, lead
pastors of Seacoast Church

"There are a few books in every generation of church leadership that end up defining and shaping a generation of leaders, and we believe this book is one of those books! In a clear, compelling, and concise way, Donna takes readers to school on what the Bible actually says about women in leadership. We believe this will set both men and women free to use their God-given gifts in new ways in the Body of Christ. Donna, thank you for enduring all you've been through to give birth to this needed and timely work. And thank you for your countless hours of study and digging into the original text to deliver an accurate and understandable discourse on biblical #sameteam leadership. It is our honor to get this book into the hands of every present and future ministry leader we know!"

**Matt and Sarah Keller**, founding and lead
pastors of Next Level Church and founders of the
Next Level Relational Network of Churches

"Donna Pisani has put her own life experience, coupled with solid theology, on the pages of this book to unleash ministries and dreams that have been hesitant or stifled. Jesus was clear that 'the harvest is great, but the laborers are few' (Luke 10). With humility and great anointed skill, these pages will equip and empower the woman who wants to be a part of the harvest work force but did not know how."

**Dr. Scott and Pastor Melanie Jones**,
lead pastors of Grace Church

# ENTRUSTED TO LEAD

—

Cultivate Your Gifts.

Build Your Confidence.

Discover Your God-Given Influence.

—

## DONNA PISANI

estherpress

Books for Courageous Women
from David C Cook

ENTRUSTED TO LEAD
Published by David C Cook
4050 Lee Vance Drive
Colorado Springs, CO 80918 U.S.A.

Integrity Music Limited, a Division of David C Cook
Brighton, East Sussex BN1 2RE, England

The website addresses recommended throughout this book are offered as a
resource to you. These websites are not intended in any way to be or imply an
endorsement on the part of David C Cook, nor do we vouch for their content.

Bible credits are listed at the back of the book. The author has
added italics to Scripture quotations for emphasis.

Library of Congress Control Number 2024938431
ISBN 978-0-8307-8728-9
eISBN 978-0-8307-8731-9

Author is represented by the literary agency of The FEDD Agency, Inc.
Post Office Box 341973, Austin, Texas 78734.

The Team: Susan McPherson, Marianne Hering, Gina Pottenger,
Karissa Silvers, Susan Murdock, Angela Messinger
Cover Design: Emily Weigel

Printed in the United States of America
First Edition 2024

1 2 3 4 5 6 7 8 9 10

*To Dennis, the love of my life and my greatest cheerleader. Leading in ministry alongside you over four decades on the #sameteam has been the greatest honor and adventure of my life. Thank you for being confident enough in your gifts to empower me in mine. I am forever grateful we get to do this together.*

# Contents

# Foreword

Writing a foreword for someone you have tremendous respect for isn't easy. Writing a foreword for a friend is even harder! Why? Because words can't quite capture relationship.

My wife, Lora, and I consider Dennis and Donna Pisani as some of our nearest and dearest friends. Leadership is lonely, in case you haven't noticed. The friendship we've shared while ministering in the same city has been a game changer! We wouldn't be who we are or where we are without them.

The introduction to this book begins with a hashtag: #sameteam. No one embodies that better than Donna. By the time you're done reading, you'll discover why we consider our friendship as one of God's great gifts to us! Donna has the gift of encouragement and empowerment.

In a world that is enamored with power and prestige, it's easy to overlook a fundamental truth: we are entrusted, not entitled, to leadership. *Entrusted to Lead* is a poignant reminder that true leadership and influence is a sacred stewardship.

At the heart of the book, Donna does a deep dive into one of God's timeless principles: the consistent inclusion and empowerment of women in leadership and influence throughout history. You'll discover the Bible is one cohesive story from the birth of humanity to the birth of the church. Donna reveals how God has used women alongside men to play pivotal roles in his redemptive plan. This is not yet another playbook on leadership techniques but rather a treasury of wisdom to ignite and challenge your leadership motivation. The bottom line? Our heart posture as leaders is the greatest predictor of our influence.

Donna shares invaluable life lessons gleaned from her leadership journey alongside her husband Dennis, providing readers with a toolbox for healthy influence and leadership. Writing with a blend of passion, humor, and vulnerability, Donna offers insights she wished she'd known earlier, in a way that will make you feel mentored, inspired, and empowered. Through the ink on the page, you will uncover and begin to cultivate your God-given entrustment as you find the confidence to use your voice as a woman to breathe life into those you're called to serve.

Whether you're a seasoned leader or embarking on your journey, the pages of this book will inspire and encourage you to leverage your God-given entrustment to impact the world around you.

*Entrusted to Lead* is more than a compilation of leadership principles—it's a roadmap for the next generation of leaders. May it fuel within you the desire to faithfully steward the leadership mantle placed on your shoulders, recognizing it not as a privilege to be grasped but an entrustment to be embraced.

Mark Batterson, *New York Times*-bestselling
author of *The Circle Maker*

# Glossary of Terms

The foundation of this book is based on a new framework and language for leadership. For clarification, here are definitions for a few key terms:

**Entitled leadership** has two aspects; it is either ego driven or insecurity driven. Entitled leadership driven by ego seeks recognition and is motivated by the pursuit of rewards, status, self-promotion, and fame. The drive for self-importance prioritizes position or title, often fueled by a sense of "you owe me," breeding ingratitude. An entitled posture driven by insecurity blinds us to what God has already entrusted us with, so our gifting remains hidden. If this leader fails to recognize the gifts entrusted to them are God-given, self-promotion will be their motivation rather than servant leadership. Entitlement magnifies a sense of insufficiency, limiting the growth of potential abilities. This is a form of *scarcity mentality* (see below) that hinders the vulnerability and authenticity necessary for leadership. Entitled leadership seeks control and power and is transactional rather than relational.

**Entrusted leadership** is rooted in humility and is driven by a deep sense of gratitude for the cost of the gifts God has given us that can transform a scarcity mentality of "not enough" to "more than enough." Entrusted influencers or leaders are not self-serving or self-promoting; instead, they model the servant leadership exemplified by Jesus (Luke 22:26). This leadership is marked by a life of surrender in which character and integrity flourish. This posture not only multiplies and nurtures God-given gifts and abilities but also relies on the empowering guidance of the Holy Spirit rather than self-reliance. Characterized by vulnerability and authenticity, it approaches leadership with curiosity without the need to protect a self-image. By embracing this posture, leaders undergo a personal transformation, embodying a life of surrender as they strive to reflect the *imago Dei*. Entrusted leadership and influence are inherently relationally driven by the desire to serve and empower others.

**Scarcity mentality** fuels an entitled leadership posture. Leaders with a scarcity mindset focus on what they lack, and as a result, they can get stuck in a "not enough" loop: an endless cycle of not enough support, not enough budget, not enough people, not enough education. Every "not enough" amplifies what we feel we're entitled to, shifts the blame, and can create ingratitude for what has already been entrusted to us. Continually operating with a scarcity mentality stymies innovation and growth, authenticity, and vulnerability. This mindset is risk-averse and has difficulty collaborating and sharing resources if there is no personal benefit.

**Incarnational leadership** results from leading with an entrusted posture. It simply means leading the way Jesus did. This leadership is fueled by the desire to reflect the life of Christ by leading in a way that imparts and transforms, not just imitates. Incarnational leaders have a passion to partner with the Holy Spirit to develop spiritual depth in those they lead rather than merely expand the width of their own personal platform. These leaders are continually honing the art of surrender rather than control.

# Introduction

## *#sameteam*

This book is an invitation.

It's an invitation for God's Word to mark your journey as we discover the leadership potential and influence God has entrusted you with.

My desire is that you will begin to not only see but believe all that God has made possible in and through you.

We've been *entrusted* with—not *entitled* to—leadership and influence, and our posture in leadership matters.

Building on the foundation of our leadership posture, this book also serves as an inspiration for women to lead alongside men, on the #sameteam, to use our unique God-given gifts together as allies.

I have been fascinated with the concept of leadership for years, reading books and listening to podcasts with a relentless curiosity for wisdom, even attaining two graduate degrees in leadership in my late fifties—seeking anything that could help me grow what I know is my God-given assignment. I wanted to be the best I could be as a woman entrusted with leadership. I didn't want the lack of confidence that consumed me to be the primary narrative of my life.

In my early days of ministry, I tried to hide my gifts because of my roaring insecurity, but my husband, thankfully, insisted we lead together and was confident enough in his own gifts to empower me in mine. His consistent prompting and encouragement gave me the courage to step up. For over forty years we've served in ministry together globally. From backpacking Bibles into the Himalayan mountains of Nepal to planting a church in our nation's capital, we endeavored to reflect the united #sameteam leadership.

Our journey has been far from perfect; volumes of books could be written on the mistakes we made while pioneering this concept of leading together in ministry. Because I was frequently the only woman at the table with few peers to model after, I had to intentionally develop leadership skills, overcome insecurity, discover my God-given gifts, and find my unique voice to communicate effectively.

Whether you are just beginning this journey of leadership or you're a weary veteran looking for encouragement, I wrote this for you. I believe my experiences and discoveries can fuel your journey with the wisdom and insights that I wish I had known when I started.

## Why *This* Book?

In today's evolving work environments, both in ministry and business, women are increasingly taking on leadership roles alongside men. However, as I sought answers to my many questions of what the dynamics could look like for healthy co-leading, I discovered a noticeable lack of resources for guidance. Numerous leadership books, historically written by men, were primarily aimed at a male audience. While these books offered valuable insight, they often overlooked the inclusion of female perspective and influence. As women began to write books on leadership in the last few decades, sadly, some conveyed a nuanced tone of anger directed at men for not creating room for their influence. My academic journey further highlighted this need for resources, as the books I discovered, while rich in the theology of men and women leading together, were extremely dense and challenging to comprehend.

I loved researching the theology regarding women and men leading together and wished I had started sooner. I didn't think I had either the time or the capacity to understand it. Yet it is necessary as a follower of Jesus to understand what God says in his story about us as women. The lens of truth we discover in God's Word will remove that nagging lie in the back of your head that makes you sometimes question whether you are qualified to lead.

This passion of mine evolved into this book, written to the girl I was thirty years ago—the girl who often wrestled with insecurity, didn't feel smart, and was not 100 percent sure she was qualified, simply because of a lack of biblical resources and practical leadership tools. I don't want another generation of young women trying to lead with blinders on, unaware of the empowerment and permission God has given them. So, this book includes theology that is easy to understand and practical ways to apply it.

On that note, the theology we'll investigate is intended for confidence, not for combat. Theology was never meant to be weaponized to defend your beliefs. I love how theologian Gordon Fee defines it: "I begin with a singular and passionate conviction: that the proper aim of all true theology is doxology. Theology that does not begin and end with worship is not biblical at all but rather is a product of western philosophy."[1] Greg Surratt, a co-founder of Association of Related

Churches and someone I consider a father in the faith, wisely suggests the need for what he calls "theological humility," which simply means keeping a posture of curiosity to learn.

While my research increased my awareness of the theological divisions among respected theologians through the centuries, and their valid points considering the cultures in which they lived, you won't find *that* debate in this book. Those differences center on the labels *complementarian* (men and women are equal in value but not in role) and *egalitarian* (men and women are equal both in value and in role).

Often differences arise when labels are used to understand ideas, but I don't think they are helpful because they divide more than unify. Perhaps it's time that rather than identifying with a label, we identify with who God knows us to be. The only label I want to be identified with is *I am a daughter of the King, made in his image, entrusted by him with gifts as I partner with him to fulfill his last words on earth: the Great Commission.*

Perhaps we've been oblivious to the obvious that the Great Commission wasn't assigned to just men but to men and women *together*. Accomplishing the Great Commission requires men *and* women to use their voices to tell the good news.

Additionally, of all the Bible verses that were fulfilled on the day of Pentecost when the church was birthed, Joel 2 was the passage Peter chose to highlight. Interesting, right? Peter's first sermon, marking the origin of the church and shaping it as we know it, empowered both men and women to use their voices together according to the gifts they were entrusted with.

Intrigued?

Good. There's more to explore. You need to know that I am not trying to convince you what to believe but to stir your curiosity and hunger to dig for yourself.

## The Foundation of Leadership

I've come to realize that although effective leadership methods are vital for organizational growth, it's our underlying heart motivation that profoundly impacts our influence. Renowned leadership expert Patrick Lencioni maintains that "leadership is a privilege,"[2] underscoring the idea that we are entrusted with authority for the sole purpose of serving others, rather than being entitled to a position.

*Entrusted or entitled.*

You'll see these two words throughout this book.

Entitled leadership is motivated by rewards and status that come from position or title.

Entrusted leadership is motivated to serve out of humility and gratitude for the gifts given to us by Christ.

While we are entitled to the promises of God, if the understanding of entrustment doesn't fuel our leadership, our motivation will become self-serving rather than to follow the leadership example Jesus lived (Luke 22:26).

Just in case no one has told you recently—or ever—we all need what God has entrusted you with.

I can't wait for you to discover it with me.

## What You'll Find

God's story from Genesis to Revelation reveals the wrestle for all of humanity: the struggle between entitlement or entrustment. My goal is to show you that the Bible is one cohesive love story; every single word is significant, showing you how cherished, valued, and empowered you are by the One who loves you most. Before we explore the cultural context and delve into the original language of the text, note that this book is separated into two sections.

Section 1: Our journey starts with the foundational theology of what God says about women leading alongside men. We begin with Jesus as the focus of our faith and what he declares over you, from the words he spoke to the way he lived. Next in Genesis with the original trust, we'll unveil the clear connection of how Jesus redeemed in the second garden what was lost in the first garden and how the power of our choices dramatically affects our God-given entrustment. And we'll discover the profound meaning behind the first name God called women. Our journey then takes us into Paul's writings, unwrapping the contested verses that have historically silenced women. You might be surprised to discover that Paul was a pioneer who empowered both women and men to collectively lead as they partnered with God to build the church.

Section 2: Within this section lies a treasure of wisdom, including insights I wish I had known when I was starting as a leader. I share four key leadership tools I acquired through some of my biggest challenges and dig into four transformative areas that proved pivotal for me: how to discover your kind of smart, how to develop the art of communication, what to do with leadership pain in order to be a healthy leader, and how to develop grit to not quit.

## The Challenge

If you're wanting to confirm what you already know or ignite a fresh passion to keep going, then perhaps this book can become a training manual for those you already influence—for the generation of leaders who are rising up around us. Let me encourage you: Help them *discover* their gifts, then *disciple* their entrustment and *deploy* them to use what the Holy Spirit has empowered them to do.

Imagine with me the unlimited possibilities of what God can do when both women and men are empowered to use their God-given entrustment and voices to partner with him in the Great Commission; the impact this can have on communities and churches is profound. The next generation of leaders might just usher in a harvest beyond anything we've ever imagined.

If you're new to this journey and are not sure you're up for the challenge, I've been praying for you, my friend, that this would encourage and inspire you and that each page would make you hungry and curious. I hope to inspire a burning curiosity that makes you desire to dig into the Bible yourself, to help you discover what you believe and make informed choices and decisions as you study the Word. All so that you have more confidence in your calling and assignment. And ultimately, so that you fall more deeply in love with Jesus, the One who loves you most.

You have so much potential—some of it yet hidden. You are entrusted by your Creator with so much gifting.

Let's uncover it together. Even if you've had no one encouraging you or cheering you on, let the words on these pages feel like oxygen to your soul.

Welcome to the journey. I'm honored to have you along.

# Hineni, Here I Am

Before we embark on our journey, let me introduce the concept of *hineni*, a Hebrew term (pronounced "hee-neh-nee") meaning "here I am." It's a moment of surrender, a pivot point that becomes a posture of transformation.

The Bible records many instances of hineni, where individuals at a crossroads in their lives chose to yield to God's plan. Our hineni is always a response to God's gracious "Here I am" first; it is never based on our performance but anchored in his goodness (Isa. 43:19). These crossroads we encounter throughout life are God's invitations to deeper connection with him. It's our surrender that flings wide the door to whatever he is offering.

Perhaps you've missed the significance of a hineni moment. Not seeing the crossroads as an invitation, you may have missed the sacred space to surrender. Adam and Eve did after the fall; they made excuses and hid in shame rather than pivoting to a posture of "Here I am."

Yet throughout the Scriptures we see the transformation that happens when we are aware of God's invitation:

Abraham (Gen. 22:11)

Jacob (Gen. 31:11; 46:2)

Moses (Ex. 3:4)

Isaiah (Isa. 6:8)

Mary (Luke 1:38)

Paul (1 Cor. 15:9–11 MSG; Eph. 3:8–11 MSG)

Each story exemplifies someone with a hineni posture of surrender in response to God's boundless grace. This is the invitation as you read the weighted words in this book, discovering page by page what God has so graciously entrusted you with. It's an invitation from the One who loves you deeply to uncover his purpose and plan at every crossroads—to pivot, to surrender, and to be marked by a hineni lifestyle.

Our response is not out of obligation but because it is the only fitting response when we remember who he is and whose we are. As the apostle Paul stated, "But because God was so gracious, so very generous, here I am. And I'm not about to let his grace go to waste" (1 Cor. 15:10 MSG). Let's not waste the costly grace by being oblivious to what God is offering in this moment.

At the end of every chapter, we will take the posture of hineni in the form of a prayer so the ink on the page marks our posture of entrustment.

# Section 1

## Chapter 1

# Oblivious to the Obvious

*It isn't that they can't see the solution. It is that they can't see the problem.*

—G. K. Chesterton

Have you ever been so tired that you just needed a few days away to breathe deeply and resuscitate your life? Go ahead and nod a silent yes if you can relate ...

Several years ago, that was my husband Dennis and me. Amid a busy life of raising four children and pastoring a thriving congregation in the heart of the nation's capital, life had become difficult and overwhelming. Each day felt as if we were walking through a minefield. Although ministry is one of the most fulfilling things you can do, it can also be stretching.

We knew we had to get away for a few days to rest and relax for a reset, so we went to a tropical paradise—just the two of us. The sound of the ocean waves and the gentle breeze eased the tension of the past season from my burdened shoulders. As Dennis and I often do when visiting a new place, we asked for popular places the locals frequented. We were told that one of the most breathtaking beaches on the island lay just minutes away from the resort. Thirty minutes later, equipped with our beach essentials, we set off in our rental car driving toward our destination. Caught up in the excitement, the realization that this stretch of sand was a *European* beach didn't give us pause; if anything it only added to the allure of the adventure.

The view did not disappoint, and the landscape of crystal clear water and white powdery sand beckoned to us. Dennis quickly found a place in the shade under a palm tree. I found a place closer to the water where the waves were breaking on the shore because I love sitting in the sun (tanned cellulite always looks better than pale white, right?). Once I got settled, I turned to check on Dennis and saw the woman sitting next to me.

She was topless!

*Maybe she just forgot her shirt today.*

I noticed the woman next to her was topless, and so was the one next to her.

We now know what a European beach is, but until that moment, we had been *oblivious to the obvious.*

I wonder how often we read the Word of God and are oblivious to the obvious truth God is speaking because we lack the full context? Let's take a deeper look at a familiar story we're often taught at Easter—a woman named Mary, who was feeling utterly hopeless and, perhaps, was oblivious to the obvious around her.

## The Second Garden

In the garden, she stood with tears streaming down her face, her heart shattered with a profound sense of grief and despair. Amid a world entangled in political and ethnic turmoil, her beloved leader had died, and she had no idea what would happen next.

The devastation was palpable ...

Had she just wasted the last three years of her life? As she ruminated over all she had experienced and seen, Mary was certain in her heart it *had* been real and that the time she had spent with him was not in vain.

The miracles.

So many miracles.

That leper who had been healed and made whole and reunited with his family. And the woman who had been bleeding for twelve years and was instantly healed the moment she touched the hem of his robes.

More than the healings, it was how he looked at and spoke to them with such tenderness. Even more than the countless lives of those who had been healed, her life, as a follower of the One who loved her unconditionally, had been turned upside down.

Jesus.

And not only her life but also the lives of her new brothers. These followers of Jesus who had been simple fishermen sustaining themselves through their daily catch were profoundly transformed and now known as fishers of men. There was no lack when Jesus was around, whether he was feeding five thousand with a boy's small lunch or finding tax money in the mouth of a fish.

She could vividly recall how all fear melted away in his presence, making everything seem possible. She could still hear the roof cracking open when the lame man had been let down from the top of the house on a stretcher and how Jesus, undisturbed, had called him "son," renaming an outcast as family. He did that often, Mary recalled; he renamed and redefined. When others were quick to label you as "less than," Jesus made you feel as if you were seen and loved immeasurably, not because of your accomplishments but simply because of who you were.

His ways were often unexpected, almost too hard to believe; this Messiah was constantly flipping the table on culture and changing religion into relationship with God. "You have heard that it was said … But I say to you …" (Matt. 5:21–22, 27–28 ESV) was how he transformed the religious ordinances that brought death into words that shed rays of life and brought illumination and freedom.

Mary thought fondly of Matthew, the local tax collector, who invited Jesus to his table with people who weren't religious. It was unheard of for a rabbi to do this! As Jesus sat there unrushed, lovingly answering their questions, he shifted a religious culture based on entitlement to one of entrusted intimacy with God.

In fact, that was one of the things she loved the most about Jesus and the very thing that he was accused of by the religious authorities: he was always sitting with people who weren't like him.

Mary knew that the table you sat at defined you and determined your status.

Jesus always attracted sinners and tax collectors and the most marginalized, but all were loved and accepted. Those who didn't feel entitled to be at the table were entrusted with profound moments and creative conversations with the One who ignited their hearts and opened their eyes to a loving Father. From the greatest influencer to the least, all felt seen and heard.

Like her.

## "Who Is It You Are Looking For?"

In this garden graveyard, Mary remembered. Tears began to well up and fall from her cheeks as she thought of how her own life had changed. When she was with him, for the first time in her life, she felt the peace of being known. He had become not only her Lord but her teacher. At a moment in time when few teachers taught deep truths to women, he took the time to teach her truths that changed the way she saw God and herself. He gave value to her as a human and as ... well, a woman.

She couldn't deny what she had seen with her own eyes and heard with her own ears, and yet this outcome was not what she expected. Or what any of them had expected. This One whom she loved so intently had been tried and found guilty as the public cried out, "Crucify him!" And then as she watched with disbelief, he was humiliated on a cross and died after uttering three words. Words that would echo throughout eternity as they shattered the darkness.

"It is finished."[1]

This One she had believed was the Messiah, the One she had given her life to follow, had died.

She couldn't believe it.

Grief-stricken, she and a few other women brought burial spices to the tomb to anoint his beloved body only to discover with astonishment that the stone, once sealing the tomb, was now rolled away, revealing an empty chamber.[2] Immediately, upon hearing Mary's recounting of the events, Peter and John raced to the tomb, confirming the empty tomb, with only Jesus' burial garments remaining. In stunned disbelief, Peter and John ran to tell the others what they had witnessed.

Yet as Mary remained, standing at the opening of the tomb, her questions began to come in waves.

*What really happened here?*

*Who took Jesus' body?*

*What does this mean for all of us who followed him?*

As she leaned into the tomb, anticipating the emptiness Peter and John had described, she blinked several times to make sure she was seeing correctly.

Before her were not one but two angels positioned at each end of where Jesus' body had lain. How breathtaking to catch this brilliant glimpse of heaven on earth, but what did it mean?

Before she could process her thoughts, the angels asked her, "Woman, why are you crying?"[3]

In complete bewilderment, Mary began to explain her grief as though they had no idea what had transpired over the last few days.

"They have taken my Lord away," Mary told them, "and I don't know where they have put him."[4]

As she spoke, she turned slowly to see someone standing next to her in the garden, not realizing it was Jesus.

He echoed the same question as the angels: "Woman, why are you crying? Who is it you are looking for?"[5]

## Gardener or God Incarnate?

The first recorded words from the lips of the resurrected Jesus were not declarations but questions. Jesus led like this.

The Gospels record more than three hundred questions he asked in the three years he walked the earth. He asked questions not because he needed answers but because we needed a course correction. His questions weren't looking for information; they were an invitation to transformation.

Thinking Jesus was the gardener, Mary responded: "Sir, if you have carried him away, tell me where you have put him, and I will get him."[6]

It's interesting to note that at first Mary thought Jesus was the gardener. Was it an obvious mistake? Maybe it wasn't a mistake at all. Could it have been a reference to the first gardener, Adam, who failed in his task to cultivate life in the garden entrusted to him? Was this "gardener," Jesus, cultivating resurrection in this graveyard, turning it into a garden teeming with life?

But perhaps Mary was oblivious to the obvious.

"Mary."[7]

It was a simple one-word response, yet he called her by name.

In a moment, she knew him. Her heart exploded. The warmth and love she had known ... the freedom from darkness she had experienced ... the love he had lavished on her broken soul ... it all came cascading over her when she heard his voice. Resurrection was woven into that one word he spoke with tender authority.

*Mary.*

She had heard him call her name so many times before; this time it was familiar and yet different. I don't know what the tone or pitch was in his voice, but I think there was a resurrection sound to it that made her come alive.

As she turned to face him, she cried out, "Rabboni!" an Aramaic word for "teacher."[8] Have we missed the significance of this response? Men had rabbis, but women were not generally educated. Yet here was Mary calling him by the name she was most acquainted with.

He was *her* teacher.

Jesus didn't correct her or say, "Mary, apparently, you've been misled. Our culture says as a woman you can't be taught deep truths. Your marginalized voice doesn't matter." No, Jesus responded with something so mind-blowing. In a moment he flipped the tables, shifted the culture, and reversed a curse.

The Bible is one story from beginning to end, one cohesive story that all fits together. It's God's story. There are no random pieces or misplaced timing.

Jesus was well aware of what he was doing in that moment in the garden.

He didn't show up to Peter and John; after the resurrection he first revealed himself to a woman.

Take a second to think that through.

It wasn't because she just happened to be in the garden doing "women's things" and there was no man available since the guys left too early. It was because God had a message for humanity, and it was imperative that he chose a woman.

Why? Because it was the woman in Genesis, Eve, who first yielded to the lie that God wasn't enough and that they were entitled to more. And although both Adam and Eve sinned by forgetting what they had been entrusted with in the garden, in one second—in another garden—Jesus reversed centuries of debate and discrimination and marginalization by appearing to a woman.

Have we been oblivious to the obvious?

Jesus said to Mary, "Don't cling to me ... for I haven't yet ascended to the Father. *But go find my brothers and tell them,* 'I am ascending to my Father and your Father, to my God and your God.'"[9]

Wait a second.

Did we just read that correctly? Did Jesus just say this to Mary, who was known for having had demons cast out of her, the same Mary who society would have said wasn't worthy or enough? Did Jesus say to *that* Mary to "go tell" her brothers that he rose from the dead?

Yes, he did.

In a culture where a woman's testimony wasn't allowed in a court of law because it held no value, a culture where women were marginalized, Jesus invited Mary to be the first to tell not only her brothers but essentially all humanity the message that is the fulcrum of history. The culmination of thousands of years of promises, the pinnacle of God's story that all the earth had been waiting for: the news that the Savior was raised from the dead to pay for our sins and redeem us from death.

Yes, he did.

Have *we* perhaps been oblivious to the obvious?

The significance of this moment can't be ignored. Because if we believe the words God speaks are inspired and breathed into with his very essence,[10] then we must believe they are still echoing over humanity today.

When God spoke, "Let there be light,"[11] an energy force was created that is still in existence today. Light travels at 186,000 miles per second; in fact, if you were to travel at the speed of light, you could travel around the earth 7.5 times in a second! Actually, the heat from the sun on your arm is an echo from the four words God spoke thousands of years ago.

There aren't expiration dates on what he speaks (like the milk in your fridge). So when Jesus said, "Go tell," those words are still alive, echoing through the centuries over you right now. Those words haven't lost any power, authority, or impetus.

So, what is it we've been entrusted with?

Resurrection.

Yes, of course, we should be telling everyone about the resurrection as a noun, an event. Yet, even more, I believe God wants us to speak about resurrection as a verb. Resurrection as a lifestyle.

You've been entrusted with resurrection in *your* mouth.

Jesus wants us to practice resurrection, to choose to see and speak life and agree with what God is already speaking over us. To be transformed by the work of *resurrection in us.*

We've been commissioned by God as women to speak resurrection over graveyards and lifeless situations. Resurrection. The same words Jesus spoke to Mary are echoing over you today, friend. They haven't weakened in their power or potential. No matter where you are on your journey, whether you are confident and filled with faith or weary and your faith has been shaken because of the battle, these words have the power to shift your perspective.

Jesus intentionally appeared to a woman first, so that you would know the value and authority on your voice as a follower of Jesus. You have a calling and an assignment of leadership alongside men as we build the kingdom of God together.

Leadership and influence are not what you've been entitled to; they're what you've been entrusted with. The Head of the church, Jesus, has entrusted you, friend, with a voice weighted with resurrection to go tell.

*Go tell.*

Those words are echoing over you right now.

And tell it we will.

## Hineni

*Here I am, Lord, standing at a crossroads. I surrender my life to you along with any hope that may seem buried in a graveyard of disappointment and discouragement. I know you are with me and that this crossroads is a garden of possibilities. Use my voice and my life to practice and speak resurrection. Open my eyes to see that you're right here with me. I whole-heartedly commit to follow you.*

Take a minute to reflect and personalize your hineni. What areas of your life have been buried in a graveyard of disappointment, hiding your potential and silencing your voice, that you need to surrender?

.............................................................................................................

.............................................................................................................

.............................................................................................................

.............................................................................................................

.............................................................................................................

.............................................................................................................

.............................................................................................................

*I say yes to all you have for me. Hineni.*

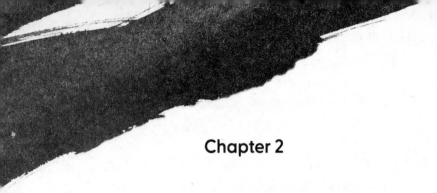

## Chapter 2

# If Mr. Giarusso
# Could See You Now

*If we are to better the future, we must disturb the present.*

—Catherine Booth

I've always felt just two brain cells short of smart.

So, the idea of furthering my education in my fifties and sixties felt like tackling an Olympian feat. I was terrified that at some point in this academic journey, someone would find out I was just a fourth grader they had let into the class, an impostor.

And yet here I was.

In my five-year academic journey, I not only had earned a master's degree in ministerial leadership but was on the verge of receiving my doctor of ministry (DMin) degree. Sharing the news of my upcoming graduation with my parents at their home in upstate New York, I emphasized that this achievement was as much theirs as it was mine, given their generous support through the years.

Sitting in their cozy living room adorned with family memories and cherished keepsakes, my eighty-five-year-old dad, usually reserved, teared up as he mentioned I would be the first in the extended family to carry the title doctor. It was the first time he ever voiced his pride in me, a deeply emotional moment adding significance to the years of hard work.

My mother's first response, however, caught me a little off guard.

"If Mr. Giarusso could see you now, Donna."

Since I didn't remember who Mr. Giarusso was, she proceeded to recall a story I had long since forgotten.

When I was a junior in high school, my grades were searing evidence of how much I hated any kind of academic rigor. I struggled with undetected ADHD and barely eked by with Cs and Ds. The only things I excelled at were art, gym, and boys. At the insistence of my parents, I went to my guidance counselor for college advice, only to discover Mr. Giarusso agreed with my hopes for the future.

"Don't worry about your grades, Donna," he advised me. "Obviously school isn't for you. Because you're so beautiful, you'll easily find a good husband, have lots of kids, and have a good life."

This was my idea of a future! I wasn't called the class flirt for nothing. As a seventeen-year-old, I was on the prowl for a good man. A "Mrs." degree was the only degree I really wanted. So, I went home, battle-ready, to confront my parents with a weapon of confirmation for this future path.

You see, Mr. Giarusso's words just validated the narrative from a childhood trauma that had been on repeat in my head. In many ways I'd had an idyllic childhood as the oldest of three children with parents who loved and cherished us. But despite this, when I was three years old, I was sexually abused by the landlord of an apartment we lived in. The landlord's words directed at me had a profound and enduring impact on me for many years; his lies tried to define me.

*It's your fault—you're just too beautiful.*
*Keep quiet because nobody will believe you.*

Those little "t" truths that were actually lies became a big "T" Truth that shaped who I thought I would always be. The sexual abuse that marked me with shame at that early age became a story that wrapped around my future. Those lies became an open door for others to feed the fear and insecurity that affected every area of my life.

*You are not enough.*
*Nobody will believe what you have to say.*
*You don't* have *a voice.*

As weird as it sounds, I was fine with settling in this space because as painful as it was, it was familiar and somewhat comfortable.

My parents were not as jubilant about Mr. Giarusso's advice as I had hoped. In fact, my mom marched into the guidance office the next day and had a few choice words with him. She saw something in me that I didn't see in myself, and she was ready to fight for it. Although she already had a good husband and three *amazing* kids, she knew that life wasn't lived in a vacuum. She knew that additional knowledge would serve me well, even if I lived the life Mr. Giarusso predicted. So as a concession, I agreed to get an associate's degree in fine arts at the local university. I couldn't possibly fail art, right?

During my second year of college, I had a life-changing experience that propelled me on a journey of healing. I discovered the tangible, boundless grace and love of God that I had yearned for; my life was completely transformed. As my relationship with Jesus deepened, it not only exposed the narrative of shame but also profoundly altered the course of my life.

That is why I can relate to Mary's story. Mary had a past and was known for her "issues" (Luke 8:2).

I wonder if when standing in the graveyard, Mary's past and present fears were loud reminders of the lies that had marked her.

Maybe that's why both of us were oblivious to the obvious.

## A Garden of Possibilities

After she saw Jesus crucified and buried, Mary's present and future looked questionable. The hope she rested in during her years of following Jesus was gone. She stood in the garden graveyard in complete bewilderment.

She was oblivious to the obvious reality that this moment was foreshadowed by the first garden—and perhaps we have been too.

I don't want you to miss the enormity of this moment.

Mary was standing in the *second* garden with Eve's seed, Jesus, who had just crushed the head of the Enemy with his death and resurrection—fulfilling the promise of redemption from the *first* garden (Gen. 3:15).

Sheesh, so powerful, hey?

There is nothing random about the details in God's story.

As a woman, I can't repeat this enough: Jesus appeared to Mary first. All of God's story for thousands of years led up to this moment ... and the rest of his story *through us* rests on this moment.

This woman and this moment, from a graveyard of dashed hopes to a garden of daring possibilities.

Perhaps you are in a moment in life where you must choose if this is a garden or a graveyard.

You decide if your story is marked by tombstones or milestones.

I had to.

We all will at some point.

For more than four decades my husband and I have had the privilege of serving in leadership roles alongside each other. While we haven't done it perfectly, we gleaned invaluable insights as we navigated challenges along the way. When we started, there weren't many women who comprehended the potential of their influence, let alone women who identified as leaders. Often I was the only female at the leadership table, navigating through the necessity to overprepare, monitor my tone, and avoid sounding too assertive. Mostly, I had to ensure that internal doubts didn't silence the potential and assignment God had given me.

The wealth of wisdom and experience I've acquired is priceless, and I wouldn't trade any of it for an easy life. I know for sure that every graveyard of past failures has the potential of becoming a garden of possibilities!

The only difference between a garden and a graveyard is what we put in the ground.

And we're the only ones who can choose to see the garden.

## The Story You Hear: Tales from the Graveyard

Maybe you weren't audibly told by someone that you don't have a voice or the potential to influence others, but the message has been on repeat in your head for so long you've accepted it.

Perhaps in the past you had something to say but you kept hearing the lie that you're just "too much," so you've kept silent.

Surely, good Christian women remain quiet and don't make waves, so just to play it safe, you've thought it best to stay passive and reserved.

Because feeling unqualified has confirmed these lies, you might not yet be convinced that the echo from Jesus' lips to "Go tell" is for you. But whatever your story, I believe by the time you finish this book, you will hear that echo loud and clear!

> The only difference between a garden and a graveyard is what we put in the ground.

Maybe you've wrestled with your confidence as I did. Or you've been sitting in the downward spiral of the fear of failure, and "I am not _____ enough" has kept you stuck.

I see you, my friend. Your story may be different from mine, but at the end of the day, you have an enemy who wants to keep you and your potential hidden. Before we begin this journey, you must realize that God is good and that his love for you is not contingent on how good you are. It's not determined by your flawlessness or capacity to adhere to any "rules." He's not keeping score or viewing our lives as a series of pass-fail tests. On the contrary, this revelation of God's unconditional love is founded on *his* grace and the good work he accomplished on the cross.

His goodness, not yours.

*We are not saved by our good works but by Christ's good work on the cross* (Eph. 2:8–9).

Before we discuss the theology of how God is for you and the fact that he gave you a voice of influence and impact as you lead alongside men, we need to consider the biblical framework for our beliefs. Let's talk about the possible lies we've believed that have kept us imprisoned or confined.

I believe that shame is the conductor of a symphony of lies that can become the soundtrack that affects every aspect of how we live our lives. It was for me. If you had told me the problem was shame, I wouldn't have believed you, mostly because I didn't understand how it operated or what it sounded like. The issue with shame's melody is it lies in disharmony with God's truth and the way his grace sounds. It is a lie that begins to shape the way you hear and see God.

If we don't see God correctly, we won't see ourselves correctly either.

## Pepper-Sprayed

For many years Dennis and I lived on Capitol Hill a few blocks from the Capitol building. A city girl at heart, I cherished every facet of life on this beloved "hill": the rich diversity, vibrant neighborhoods, the many delightful restaurants, and coffee shop options. Yet, living in a row house came with its challenges; street parking, in particular, was a perpetual headache. (Our parking tickets could have funded a small nation!)

One evening, as part of our weekly date-night ritual, Dennis and I prepared to head out. As we approached the car, Dennis produced a small canister.

"What's that?" I inquired.

"It's pepper spray," he replied, citing a recent uptick in carjackings in our neighborhood. "You need to pay attention. I'm stashing this in your car just in case you ever need it."

Even as he spoke, I found myself only half listening, as I was more concerned about reaching our reservation on time. Oblivious to his demonstration, I continued walking, missing his instructions entirely. Unbeknownst to me, he had already activated the button on the canister. Stepping into the street, I walked straight into the swirling cloud of pepper spray, instantaneously engulfed in searing pain and blindness. Amid the clamor of honking cars urging me to safety, my husband rushed to protect me from the oncoming traffic, only to stumble into the same cloud of pepper spray himself! Blinded and disoriented, we groped our way back to the house to recover. We laugh about it now, but it makes me wonder how many of us have experienced our own version of being "pepper-sprayed."

In many ways, shame is like pepper spray. We keep it close for protection because it can make us feel safe, but it blinds us to what we are really missing: a life of purehearted vulnerability and a deep relationship with God and others.

Shame makes us hide the parts of us where God is most present.

The underpinning of shame is a scarcity mentality that tells us we are not enough.

It is fascinating to me that the initial description of the first two humans, Adam and Eve, is that they "were both naked, and they *felt no shame*" (Gen. 2:25). Such an interesting choice of words, don't you think? God could have chosen any terms to describe the human condition at this moment. Why, then, is "no shame" the first ones he used?

Why not say they were happy, content, strong, and confident, or that they felt no fear, no anger or sadness or disappointment or regret? Because perhaps this was God's original design for his creation: *no shame*. I believe God knew this would be one of the primary struggles for all humanity.

Shame robs us of a vulnerable relationship with God and others, steals our identity, and blinds us to our purpose.

Shame's lies dictate to us that we must achieve perfection, deliver a flawless performance, and tirelessly strive to please God. All the while, God is standing with outstretched arms, inviting us into his grace, desiring a vulnerable, intimate relationship with us.

Remember God is good and loves you, not *in spite* of your imperfections but *because of* them. He's already paid the price for all past, present, and future failures ... everything shame wants you to hide.

Perhaps we've all been "pepper-sprayed."

And in the process, we've been oblivious to the obvious.

You've heard it said that what you don't know can't hurt you. But it can hurt you, like the pepper spray that blinds you to the truth.

The truth remains: Regardless of the graveyard of dashed hope you've encountered, God will transform it into a garden if you let him.

All those failures and obstacles you've encountered in the past are not tombstones meant to stop you. They are milestones meant to strengthen you.

## Your Own Kind of Smart

Let's revisit the question I asked in chapter 1: *Have we been oblivious to the obvious echo from Jesus?*

I was, and maybe you have been too.

As we embark on this journey, I want you to feel "mentored" through the pages of this book. I want you to feel the permission and freedom to embrace and cultivate your God-given calling and assignment with confidence and affirmation, knowing you're not alone.

I believe in you, but more importantly, so does God.

If you can learn from my life lessons and hear a spiritual mama speaking to you, it might not take you as long as it took me.

## Hineni

*Here I am, God. I give you my story, the places where shame and scarcity have been trying to hide the areas where you are most present, where the lies have been louder than the truth.*

Take a minute to reflect and personalize your hineni. Where have the lies of shame and scarcity become louder than the truth in your life?

.......................................................................................................

.......................................................................................................

.......................................................................................................

.......................................................................................................

.......................................................................................................

.......................................................................................................

.......................................................................................................

.......................................................................................................

*I say yes to all you have for me. Hineni.*

## Chapter 3

# Ground Zero: Understanding Your Leadership Entrustment

*The way we deal with uncertainty says a lot about whether Jesus is ahead of us leading or behind us just carrying our stuff.*

—Bob Goff

For decades, I have been captivated with the concept of leadership.

In the previous chapter you caught a glimpse of my personal journey. Refusing to feel two brain cells short of smart for the rest of my life, I became driven by an insatiable curiosity to learn everything I could about leadership. I was determined to grow so that fear and insecurity around my own inadequacies didn't hinder my calling and assignment from God.

I consumed the latest podcasts, devoured the newest books from leadership gurus, and asked a million questions of any leader willing to respond. In my relentless pursuit to become the best leader I could be, I certainly didn't navigate things perfectly. However, if I can share some wisdom I've learned, perhaps it will help you establish a solid foundation.

As I pondered specifically what to include related to women leading alongside men and wrestled with which aspects to focus on, one crucial element emerged: *motivation* over *methodology*. In other words, the heart motivation of *why* we want to lead rather than the methods of *how* to lead. Over the years, I've come to realize that while a brilliant methodology is important, it's your motivation for leading that truly shapes your influence. In fact, your motivation serves as a more significant predictor of the fruit of your success than the most exceptional methodology ever will.

Patrick Lencioni, a well-known leadership and organizational-health guru, underscores the pivotal nature of this concept in his book *The Motive*. He maintains that "there are only two motives that drive people to become a leader. First, they want to serve others, to do whatever is necessary to bring about something good for the people they lead. They understand that sacrifice and suffering are inevitable in this pursuit and that serving others is the only valid motivation for leadership."[1] The second motive is because "they want to be rewarded ... and are drawn by its trappings: attention, status, power, money."[2] Lencioni concludes that "leadership is a privilege,"[3] implying that leaders are entrusted with authority for the single purpose of serving others.

Throughout our journey, one pivotal question will emerge repeatedly: Is our motivation to lead kindled by entitlement or rooted in entrustment? Do we feel entitled to a title, position, or rewards, or do we embrace the sacred entrustment of God-given gifts to serve others? Our answer profoundly impacts and shapes our journey because leadership is not solely about our position but about the purpose behind it.

This ongoing inner struggle is a timeless challenge, one I've wrestled with throughout my life and one we'll discover is common to humanity, reaching all the way back to the first garden. (More on this in chapter 5.) Before we delve into the theology of women leading alongside men or explore and refine our God-given gifts, it's crucial to firmly grasp the foundation of the influence we've been granted. The greatest temptation we all face is to lose sight of the value and profound significance of what has been entrusted to us. When this happens, our sense of entitlement slips in. Rather than remaining grounded in our sense of entrustment that yields long-lasting fruitfulness, we allow our methodology to steer our influence.

Understanding the value of something determines how we guard it.

Take, for instance, the delight we all feel discovering hidden treasures. One television show that gave our family endless hours of entertainment was *Antiques Roadshow*. The PBS program features experts who appraise antiques brought in by hope-filled people. Each episode unveils surprising discoveries, revealing that items once considered household clutter were, in fact, hidden treasures.

Watching this show would invariably inspire one of our four kids to bring us a cherished toy, begging us to take it to an antique dealer, utterly convinced it held genuine value. Of course, we knew that the Woody doll with one arm hanging by a thread or the Cabbage Patch Kids doll with love notes written in permanent marker on her face was in fact only valuable to our children. The value of anything is in how you see it.

I vividly remember one particular episode of the show that made a stop in Corpus Christi, Texas. A man presented a Diego Rivera painting that had been hanging for decades in an obscure location in his family home. Diego Rivera, whom the appraiser called "arguably one of the most important Latin American twentieth-century artists,"[4] was only eighteen years old when he painted *El Albañil*. The piece, considered one of Rivera's earliest paintings, had been missing for years. This man's painting was authenticated as *El Albañil* and appraised at eight hundred thousand to one million dollars!

Needless to say, the painting's owner was gleefully shocked. He carried the painting out of the *Antiques Roadshow* program with much care—completely different from how he had brought it in. The only difference was that he had discovered the value of the painting that had been entrusted to him. From that moment on, this treasure was closely guarded.

I find myself wondering how often we become overly familiar with the masterpiece God has entrusted *in us*, unintentionally leaving it unguarded and vulnerable to theft.

## Guarding the Entrustment

During a period of intense persecution, Timothy, who led the church in Ephesus, received profound guidance from his mentor, Paul, who urged him to "guard the good deposit that was entrusted to you" (2 Tim. 1:14). Turmoil and persecution had reached alarming levels, as Nero blamed Christians for the devastating fire in Rome that had destroyed half the city in AD 64. Timothy was grappling with a multitude of challenges in his church plant, where persecution and internal divisions posed a significant threat to God's work. His spiritual father, Paul—no stranger to adversity—wrote the above advice to Timothy from a prison shortly before his death. Drawing from his own experiences, Paul understood the vital importance for Timothy as a leader and influencer to safeguard his God-given entrustment and calling, knowing that in the midst of adversity, the temptation to lose sight of it would be strong.

If Paul were alive today, I wonder if we'd be getting a letter too!

The amount of division and criticism on social media, the lack of trust in leadership, and the pain, offense, and trauma we've faced just in the last decade have all created the perfect storm, setting the stage for God to move. Yet, as Paul instructed Timothy, it's often during the most challenging moments of the battle that we tend to overlook the need to guard our entrusted gifts; insecurity can creep in, and we feel "less than" when we measure ourselves against those who are achieving the success we hoped for. In this state, the temptation to quit and harbor feelings of entitlement, thinking that "God owes me," can take hold and cause a significant shift in our perspective and leadership motivation.

But you're not alone in this, friend. At some point, we each encounter this common test of leadership to assess our motives.

To gain a clearer understanding of what could be motivating us, let's start by delving deeper. The entitled posture has two aspects: one is driven by ego and the other by insecurity. If you're ego driven, you seek recognition and are motivated by the pursuit of rewards, status, self-promotion, and fame. This self-centered approach is fueled by a sense of "you owe me," which nurtures an ungrateful attitude. If you're driven by insecurity, it may seem easier to conceal your God-given gifts because you're convinced by fear that you lack the necessary qualities to lead.

This version of entitlement (based on the fear of "not enough") can also be described as a scarcity mentality because it is fixated on deficiencies rather than gifts. The recurring refrain, *I am not* _____ *enough* or *If only I had more* _____ *or were more* _____, *then I could accomplish my purpose* amplifies what we believe we're entitled to and ultimately blinds us to what we've already been entrusted with by God, so our gifting remains hidden. Entitled leadership and influence can be described as transactional in nature and sometimes results in attempts to control and manipulate others.

Although we are entitled to all God has in store for us, we must first be rooted in a posture of entrustment, or we risk losing sight of the why, the purpose behind the gifts and assignments we've been given by God.

The entrusted posture is rooted in humility and is driven by a deep sense of gratitude for our God-given gifts that can transform a scarcity mentality into a "more than enough" mindset. Entrusted leaders fully acknowledge that God is the source of their gifts and that the cost of this invaluable entrustment was the ultimate sacrifice of Jesus on the cross. Entrusted influencers or leaders are not self-serving or self-promoting; instead, they model the servant leadership exemplified by Jesus (Luke 22:26). This leadership is marked by a life of surrender in which character and integrity flourish. Entrusted leadership and influence are inherently relationally driven by the desire to serve and empower others.

There is vast difference between entitled and entrusted leadership:

One feeds our ego; the other breeds humility.

One is ungrateful; the other is deeply grateful.

One limits our potential and abilities; the other multiplies our abilities as we use them.

One is defensive and makes excuses; the other is vulnerable and authentic.

One blames others for failure; the other is curious to grow from failure and craves feedback.

You can't be breathing and not have battled a sense of entitlement in one way or another. It's when leadership is hard and you feel God owes you more. Or when you feel as if your team, spouse, family, or the world owes you more. It's easy to forget that your position of influence is a God entrustment when he doesn't move fast enough or the way you want. The battle intensifies when the temptation to control the outcome becomes irresistible. Perhaps like me, you have to fight a sense of entitlement when you're scrolling on social media and you start comparing what's missing in your behind-the-scenes life to someone else's carefully curated highlight reel. Before you realize it, you've lost sight of your own entrusted gifts because you feel entitled to more of whatever they appear to have.

I don't know about you, but this has been my story during the particularly challenging moments of leadership. Throughout my life, I have wrestled with maintaining a perspective that prevents my ego or insecurity from turning the invaluable entrustment from God into a sense of entitlement. Perhaps you have had to face an intense battle, and you had no idea until now that it was intended to solidify your heart's motivation for leadership and influence.

At the end of the day, *how* you see what you've been entrusted with determines your influence.

## A Slight Perspective Change Affects Everything

It wasn't too long ago that I went to get new prescription glasses. Driving home, I became aware of how crisp everything felt and looked. I even remarked to my husband that it was a pleasant day because it was so "clear." What I had failed to recognize was that the clarity I was experiencing wasn't because the air was clear but because I was seeing the world through my new prescription lenses.

I wonder how many of us are going along in life with an old prescription that no longer suits us? Consistently trying to see through an old lens smudged with fears or lack of knowledge that keeps us pigeonholed.

Perhaps that's where you are right now. Maybe you need a new "prescription" to see your leadership or influence with a new perspective. No doubt, it's time to stop allowing a sense of entitlement to keep you from using the entrustment you already have. Ultimately, this isn't about us; it's about the people God intends to impact through the gifts he's given us.

You, my friend, have been entrusted with unique gifts from the One who loves you most. Now that we've laid the groundwork to better understand our motivation, let's keep going. There's more you need to better equip you for your journey.

## A New Way to Lead

Over the years I came to realize the concept of women co-leading with men encompasses numerous aspects. While each aspect is crucial to highlight, I had to identify the starting point, the ground zero for me personally. During a lecture from my mentor, Dr. Leonard Sweet, I experienced a profound shift in perspective that fundamentally transformed my understanding.

"My identity is not as a leader. It is found as a follower of Jesus," Dr. Sweet maintained. "Identity is found in followership. Sometimes

I am summoned to the front of the line to use the function of leadership."[5] My first response to this idea, if I'm honest, was irritation. I had spent decades identifying and building my leadership gifts, because, after all, everything rises and falls on the strength of a leader, right?

But as I further explored Dr. Sweet's perspective, I uncovered a fascinating revelation: the term *leader* appears only four times in the New Testament, while *follower* is mentioned more than forty times! How had I not seen this before? Perhaps in God's perspective, the concept of following is ten times more significant than leading! Clearly this insight doesn't diminish the importance of leadership; rather, it issues a caveat that we can only lead well if we first follow well.

Although following Jesus is Christianity 101, I had an aha moment when I realized that we do not just need stronger leaders; we need to relearn that we are followers *first*. The modern church (me included) has become consumed with leadership and influence, but we have it backward. Dealing with the past decade of leadership failures, a generation deconstructing the church and their faith, and a pandemic demands a shift in our perspective on leadership and influence. If I'm honest, I thought I *was* following first, but I realized in the most challenging aspects of leadership, I was not dedicating as much time developing my followership as I was my leadership. It is not one or the other; it is both. It is only by following well that we grasp the authentic nature of leadership.

## Honing the Art of Followership

So then, maybe entrusted influence begins with honing the art of followership.

Could it be that effectively leading or influencing like Jesus comes from first becoming like him and developing an entrusted servant's heart? As we follow Jesus and mature as a disciple, we move beyond just imitating him and become genuinely transformed—by his words and his character.

At its core, the aim of our leadership is *incarnational*. Simply put, the more intentional we are at becoming intimately acquainted with him and deepening our relationship with him, the more we begin to think, live, and influence as he did.

I don't think we drift into a lead-first, follow-second mentality intentionally.

Perhaps we need to be aware that the enemy of followership is entitlement. And when entitlement is the seat we're sitting in at the leadership table, we want control, navigating our leadership in our own strength.

Any other recovering control freaks like me? I can totally relate to this; some days I am more recovered than others!

Listening and following.

It's not rocket science. Even the wind and the waves follow him. Light has followed his direction since the beginning of time ...

But the million-dollar question right now is "Are we following him?"

My answer to that question depends on the day I'm asked. I can say at a superficial level, "Of course, I am following Jesus!" But there are many days when I am not 100 percent following because there is still 25 percent of me that wants to be in control, driving precariously toward *my* desired outcome, which is not always his!

I know I am not the only one struggling with this because it's one of the greatest leadership lessons Jesus had to teach his followers, one that would mark their leadership journey for the rest of their lives.

## Ahead of Us or behind Us

In the sixteenth chapter of Matthew, a pivotal moment for the disciples unfolded as Jesus led them to Caesarea Philippi, a city nestled at the base of Mount Hermon. This ancient city, where the locals worshipped Greek gods at numerous shrines, was one of Palestine's most pagan strongholds. Jesus was brilliant at illustrating his message, not only through the words he spoke but also by the physical settings where he taught. It was no mere coincidence that he was standing in a place often referred to as the Gates of Hell as he aimed to leave a lasting impression. He wanted all who were following him to unequivocally understand his identity.

"Who do people say the Son of Man is?" Jesus asked (v. 13).

None of the disciples realized this was a defining moment in their journey with him.

"Who do *you* say I am?" Jesus asked (v. 15).

Nor did they realize how these two questions would shape their calling and purpose over the rest of their lives. I wonder how often they would recall this moment as they led the first-century church.

Simon Peter's rare moment of brilliance was divinely inspired as he answered, "You are the Messiah, the Son of the living God" (v. 16).

Jesus' response to Peter is astounding:

> You are blessed, Simon son of John, because my
> Father in heaven has revealed this to you. You did

not learn this from any human being. Now I say to you that you are Peter (which means "rock"), and upon this rock I will build my church, and all the powers of hell will not conquer it. And I will give you the keys of the Kingdom of Heaven. Whatever you forbid on earth will be forbidden in heaven, and whatever you permit on earth will be permitted in heaven. (vv. 17–19 NLT)

Whew, let's not miss this point.

Jesus not only commended Peter for the rock-solid revelation, but, based on that revelation, gave him his identity, Peter, which means "rock." Then he's given authority, the keys to the kingdom.

The key to fully comprehending *your* identity and authority lies in knowing who Jesus is.

Let me repeat that. Your identity and authority come only in knowing who Christ is *first*.

Peter had no idea that the purpose God had for his life was to lead the early church in the days to come, nor did he have any idea that the Rabbi was giving him a Leadership 101 lesson. Jesus wanted Peter to remember this moment as they stood in front of the Gates of Hell where other gods were worshipped. Perhaps Jesus was telling Peter:

> *"This is ground zero, the place where you'll keep the core of your leadership, and it's not a physical place but a revelation and a posture. This is the foundation to find your identity and authority as you fulfill your purpose*

*in the future. Because this is the rock-solid revelation you'll need and use to build my church.*

*"If you hold on to this one revelation, all the powers of hell you'll face in the future will not conquer it."*

The sheer empowerment in this revelation is massive.

Peter couldn't believe it! Finally, despite his emotional outbursts and doubt of himself and others, he had received this life-changing shout-out from the Rabbi. Not only had he answered one of Jesus' many questions with the right answer, but Jesus also said it was a rock-solid answer that he would use to build the church. Then on top of that, Jesus gave him the keys to the kingdom!

I can't help but wonder if Peter was already contemplating whether it might be too soon to start printing those commemorative T-shirts, envisioning *#winning* boldly emblazoned across the front ...

Yeah, maybe too soon.

Because that wasn't the end of the story or the leadership lesson.

Jesus repeatedly cautioned his disciples about the inevitability of his journey to Jerusalem, where he would suffer, be crucified, and rise again on the third day. It served as a spoiler alert so they wouldn't be caught off guard. Despite his repeated warnings, they struggled to fully grasp the significance of his words because daily they witnessed the miraculous unfolding before their eyes. Hundreds were being healed and becoming followers of Jesus; even as the persecution intensified, the crowds grew. The disciples were astounded by the extraordinary days they were living in!

At one point, as Jesus reiterated the challenges awaiting him in Jerusalem, Peter quietly pulled Jesus aside. Feeling the confidence from his last winning response, Peter said, "Never, Lord! ... This shall never happen to you!" (Matt. 16:22).

Turning to Peter, Jesus immediately responded, "Get behind me, Satan! You are a stumbling block to me; you do not have in mind the concerns of God, but merely human concerns" (v. 23).

Wait a second, did Jesus just call Peter "Satan"?!

I don't believe so. I think he was naming what Peter suggested—a lie from Satan—and *that* was the stumbling block.

Peter went from a revelation that was rock-solid to one that was a stumbling block!

Jesus was acutely aware that Peter had to master this lesson well. To fully live out the leadership he would be entrusted with after Jesus' resurrection, Peter would need to remember this one thing explicitly.

And it's the one thing *we* need to remember explicitly.

What did Jesus say first? The answer to that question sets up the rest of what he said.

"Get *behind* me ..."

This tells me Peter was *in front* of Jesus, trying to lead rather than follow, when the very first invitation and calling on Peter's life from Jesus was to "follow me" (v. 4:19).

As I zoom out on this story, I can totally relate to Peter.

Jesus had been telling them he was going to suffer and be crucified. Perhaps Peter felt more comfortable following Jesus when he was the Messiah, the powerful Son of the living God, the one performing miracles in front of a huge crowd. No one really knew who Peter was before Jesus; he was just a fisherman. Now he had influence and was known. He liked following *that* Jesus.

But when Jesus was going to show up as the suffering Savior, Peter wasn't as comfortable with *that* image of God.

Perhaps Peter is like us. I am fine when God shows up in a way I'm comfortable with: the Miracle Worker, the powerful God, the One who answers my prayers when I need him to and the way I want him to. But when he doesn't, I want to control the situation, and before I know it, I have stopped following and started leading.

> *Hmm ... I don't see any hope for positive outcomes, so I will step up for just a minute.*

> *This is taking longer than I anticipated. Let me help God and figure this out myself.*

> *I hate feeling as if I am not in control, and this clearly feels as if I am not.*

> *I am feeling entitled to a different answer, so I'll get back to following once I have clarity.*

When we do this, we go from having a rock-solid revelation to becoming our own stumbling blocks. In the process, we lose our identity and base our authority on our giftings and experience. And our leadership shifts from entrusted to entitled. It's difficult to expect God to lead us if we've already decided on where we think we should go.

This story ends with a profound revelation. I love how Eugene Peterson phrases it:

> Then Jesus went to work on his disciples. "Anyone who intends to come with me has to let me lead. You're not in the driver's seat; *I* am. Don't run from suffering; embrace it. Follow me and I'll show you how. Self-help is no help at all. Self-sacrifice is the way, my way, to finding yourself, your true self. What kind of deal is it to get everything you want but lose yourself? What could you ever trade your soul for?" (Matt. 16:24–26 MSG)

Entitled or entrusted leadership and influence is determined by *who* is in the driver's seat. Or as Bob Goff says, "The way we deal with uncertainty says a lot about whether Jesus is ahead of us leading or behind us just carrying our stuff."[6]

It was the entrusted leadership posture Jesus modeled when he said:

> You know that the rulers of the Gentiles lord it over them, and their high officials exercise authority over them. Not so with you. Instead, whoever wants to become great among you must be your servant, and whoever wants to be first must be your slave—just as the Son of Man *did not come to be served, but to serve,* and to give his life as a ransom for many. (20:25–28)

In the middle of a lively argument between the disciples about who would be the greatest, Jesus' response was clear: Leadership, ministry, or influence is not about position and authority. It's about servanthood, *first*.

We lead as we follow and serve.

In other words, our calling is to follow, and our assignment is *servant* leadership.

Because if serving is below you, leadership is beyond you.

Followership is our base of authority and identity. Even at the last meal Jesus had with his disciples, the final message he left them reflects this. After he had served them by washing their feet, he asked them, "Do you understand what I have done for you?" (John 13:12).

I think this same message is echoing over you right now as you read this.

"Do you understand what I've done for you? The cost of what I am entrusting to you?"

> ## Because if serving is below you, leadership is beyond you.

So, before we get into the rest of the book, maybe it's time to take a moment to surrender to God the areas of your life where you feel entitled. Think about the moments when you feel the most entitled with "you owe me" thoughts. When you take back control because of hurts or fears. When you feel not enough or not seen. When your ego says that you deserve more honor or that nobody appreciates what you do for them.

Now take those moments and bring them to the feet of Jesus. Answer his questions for yourself.

"Who do *you* say I am?"

Go ahead. Who is Jesus to you?

"Do you understand what I have done for you?"

It's a question we need to answer every day for the rest of our lives.

## Hineni

*Here am I, Lord. I surrender to you the areas of entitlement due to ego, insecurity, and scarcity mentality. I am grateful for your entrustment— the cost you paid. Forgive me for leading without following first.*

Take a moment to personalize your hineni prayer of surrender. In what areas have entitlement or scarcity mentality been shaping your leadership or influence?

........................................................................................

........................................................................................

........................................................................................

........................................................................................

........................................................................................

........................................................................................

........................................................................................

........................................................................................

*I say yes to all you have for me. Hineni.*

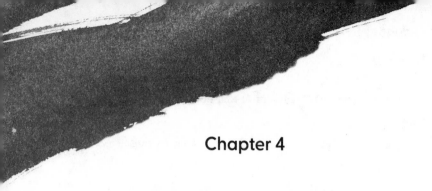

## Chapter 4

# The Jesus Echo

*There is no erasing a woman whose life tells "his" story.*

—Ann Voskamp

The most extraordinary archaeological discoveries are frequently shrouded in darkness, entombed beneath layers of soil, concealed for centuries still awaiting discovery. As a child, one of my cherished pastimes was poring over the *National Geographic* magazines that my grandfather generously gifted our family. I was always intrigued by hidden archaeological treasures and the wealth of knowledge they revealed as they were unearthed. My brainwaves still start percolating when I dive into the captivating history of a civilization from the distant past. As archaeologists meticulously follow the trail of clues and methodically excavate treasures under layers of dirt, we get a glimpse of God's fingerprints throughout history. This insight so often changes the narrative we once knew, adding a richness and depth that we had missed.

We are going to do some excavation in the next few chapters, dusting off some truth that perhaps has been buried for far too long.

It just may be that we've missed God's fingerprints, his clues, or evidence of the entrusted leadership and influence he's given to women that's woven throughout the tapestry of the Gospels simply because we haven't understood the cultural context.

A. W. Tozer wrote in *The Knowledge of the Holy* that "our real idea of God may lie buried under the rubbish of conventional religious notions and may require an intelligent and vigorous search before it is finally unearthed and exposed for what it is."[1] Let's put Tozer's advice into practice and dust off some of those *conventional religious notions* to dig beneath the surface of what has been traditionally taught about women.

So welcome to class! Get ready for "an intelligent and vigorous" look at Scripture. Grab a pen to underline and write notes in the margins. I believe a book should be marked by the marks it's making on us personally. Those notes might become a field manual for your future and a road map for others who will be impacted by your influence.

I believe you'll discover, as I did, there is a wealth of evidence revealing how Jesus sees and values women and our voices. Maybe like Mary in the garden, we have been oblivious to the obvious.

I love how the renowned English writer Dorothy L. Sayers summarizes Jesus' view of women:

> Perhaps it is no wonder that the women were first at the Cradle and last at the Cross. They had never known a man like this Man—there never has been such another. A prophet and teacher who never nagged at them, never flattered or coaxed or

patronised; who never made arch jokes about them, never treated them either as "The women, God help us!" or "The ladies, God bless them!"; who rebuked without querulousness and praised without conde-scension; who took their questions and arguments seriously; who never mapped out their sphere for them, never urged them to be feminine or jeered at them for being female; who had no axe to grind and no uneasy male dignity to defend; who took them as he found them and was completely unself-conscious. There is no act, no sermon, no parable in the whole Gospel that borrows its pungency from female per-versity; nobody could possibly guess from the words and deeds of Jesus that there was anything "funny" about woman's nature.[2]

Dorothy got it right. Who *wouldn't* want to follow someone who believes in them and is their biggest champion?

Perhaps you've wrestled with the notion that your contributions are inadequate or that you've yet to unearth your true potential. As we begin to excavate and dust off the hidden treasures in the Bible, I can't wait for you to discover the compelling evidence of how you are seen and cherished. There are moments in life when, like Mary in the garden, we stand perplexed and in need of a gentle reminder. Moments when Jesus' first words to her—"Who are you looking for?"—serve as a compass guiding us back to our starting point. My hope is that you see Jesus championing not only your humanity but, more importantly, your identity as a woman as well.

## The Most Valuable Player

Often when we want to develop our understanding of the biblical role of women, we start with the most contentious passages on gender roles: Paul's letters to the early church. However, diving into those passages first would be like jumping into the middle of the story, not beginning at the starting point. (We will wait until chapters 6 and 7 to look at those passages.) When using GPS to find our way to a destination, none of us would insert the journey's halfway point as the starting point. Yet when it comes to the theology of women leading alongside men, that's what we've done—started in the middle and overlooked the starting point.

As we dive into the theology of women leading alongside men, I don't want us to miss the MVP of our story: Jesus.

In essence, we must begin with the profound significance that Jesus attributed to women and how he treated them. As Jesus is the foundation of our faith, it's crucial to consider how he regarded women within the cultural context of his time rather than fitting him into a religious framework shaped by our *contemporary* culture. My goal is to encourage you by emphasizing the central role that women play alongside men in the arc of God's redemptive story.

As you read, I hope you'll see how Jesus' words and actions echo the value he places on you as a woman, helping you recognize the evidence that marks your journey.

## Jesus Was Revolutionary

Before we embark on an excavation of the Gospels, it's essential to recognize that Jesus lived in a culture different from our own. Men exclusively held significant power. In contrast, women, children, and slaves were disempowered and devoid of rights, value, and a voice in society. The laws and court system of that period further reinforced this perspective.

Jesus challenged this first-century culture's diminished view of women by seeing their value when they were typically unseen. As we dig into how Jesus treated women, we'll discover his posture was not only inclusive but empowering. He challenged the prevailing legal, cultural, and religious norms by treating women as people whose value and significance was equal to that of men.[3] I don't want us to miss the revolutionary cultural shifts Jesus practiced as a rabbi as he both validated and elevated the marginalized: foreigners, slaves, children, and women.

If you've lacked exposure to the historical context, you might miss the profound significance, as I initially did. H. Wayne House, a leading evangelical scholar, writes, "Jesus treated women with kindness and respect and considered them equal before God," and he treated women as though they were "*of equal intelligence, equal spiritual discernment, and equal religious acumen.*"[4]

Jesus didn't consider women two brain cells short of smart!

Rob Dixon writes, "How Jesus treated women was a significant corrective to how men treated women in first-century Jewish culture."[5] Mary J. Evans, co-editor of *The IVP Women's Bible Commentary*, adds, "We must take care in assessing the impact of Jesus' approach ... not to forget just how *revolutionary* it was."[6]

Don't miss this: The way Jesus treated women was and still is revolutionary!

Additionally, the inclusion of women in the Gospels offers a stark departure from the portrayal of women in ancient Greek, Roman, and

Jewish literature where women were talked about but seldom given a voice.[7] Remarkably, the gospels Matthew, Mark, and Luke alone highlight women in 112 distinct passages.[8]

Have we perhaps been oblivious to how significant it is that Jesus treated all women with dignity?[9] In fact, nowhere in the Gospels do you find Jesus prohibiting women from leadership by what he says, nor does he ever imply that only men can be leaders.[10] Surprised by this? You might be thinking, "What about the twelve male apostles?" Don't worry, we'll get to that. Whether this realization encourages or unsettles you, particularly if it challenges your established theology, I urge you to continue reading.

## Jesus Chose to Include Women in His Story

*The family tree of Jesus Christ, David's son, Abraham's son ...*
—Matthew 1:1 MSG

In my early days as a Christian, when I set off to read through the New Testament, I would often skip the first chapter of Matthew—Jesus' genealogy—because, well, it was boring. Honestly, who cares about these people? You might have skipped to the inspiring parts too, yet nothing God does is random or without intentionality. Everything he does deserves our attention.

These genealogies held immense significance and served as a kind of resume. They were frequently used to establish the honorable lineage a person came from. It was common practice to conceal the existence of undesirable individuals while highlighting the virtues of the noble ones.

However, Jesus' genealogy did the complete opposite. Matthew intentionally included the most unlikely figures, individuals you'd typically prefer to keep hidden: murderers, cheats, and people like your crazy uncle no one talks about.

Even more intriguing is that although genealogies at the time typically excluded women, Jesus' family line features not just one but five significant women: Tamar, Rahab, Ruth, Bathsheba, and Mary. These women, despite their low social status, influenced the course of history though their courageous lives. Ordinary, everyday women, much like us, trying to navigate life while facing challenges, the least likely to be chosen for Jesus' family tree. But they were integral to his story, just as we are—imperfect but not hidden. Jesus' groundbreaking "resume" looked different from other rabbis' because he wanted everyone for all time to know the fruit of his family tree was the redemption of both men *and* women, regardless of background. Jesus challenged prejudice and bias by elevating the status of women. He emphasized that women were central, not just secondary beneficiaries of his trust and teachings, by giving women a significant place in his story, and that includes you!

## Jesus Leveled the Playing Field

> *"Teacher," they said to Jesus, "this woman was*
> *caught in the act of adultery. The law of Moses*
> *says to stone her. What do you say?"*
>
> —John 8:4–5 NLT

As we dig further to grasp the cultural context of Scripture, even the most familiar Bible stories gain depth. Early one morning, as Jesus began teaching at the Temple Mount, a growing crowd swarmed around him, eager to hear from him. However, the atmosphere suddenly shifted when the religious scholars and Pharisees thrust a terrified, trembling woman caught in the act of adultery to the forefront, interrupting him (John 8:1–11).

They hoped to ensnare Jesus by coaxing a statement from him they could later use against him, but Jesus simply stooped down and started writing in the dirt with his finger. I can hardly fathom the depth of humiliation the woman must have experienced being forcibly dragged to the temple square disheveled and exposed, awaiting her judgment.

And if you're anything like me, you may have pondered why it was only the woman whom the religious leaders thrust into the spotlight. The last time I checked, adultery involves *two* people, so where was the man? In fact, our Bibles often title this story "The Woman Caught in Adultery." If these male religious leaders were so fervent about upholding the law, why did they neglect to bring the man forward as well? According to the law they were so intent on enforcing, both the man and the woman involved in adultery were subject to the penalty of death (Lev. 20:10; Deut. 22:22). Perhaps their actions were influenced by a culture that not only devalued women but, in the case of adultery, frequently presumed that women bore the primary responsibility for the act of infidelity.

Jesus was acutely aware of the glaring double standard at play, and he steadfastly refused to buy into it. We may never know the specifics of what he was writing in the dirt, but the words he spoke next were weighted with a truth that blew the dust off, exposing the biases of the religious culture.

"Let any one of you who is without sin be the first to throw a stone at her" (John 8:7). Stripped bare by the conviction of his words, one by one, beginning with the eldest, the men quietly stole away. When Jesus and the woman were the only ones left, his final words to her were "Go and sin no more" (v. 11 NLT). Jesus wasn't endorsing her actions; instead, he was leveling the playing field. Regardless of gender, accountability was paramount.

The men pointed their accusatory fingers at the woman as the problem, but instead of using his finger to accuse, Jesus beckoned her with an invitation to experience his love, truth, and mercy. He conveyed a profound understanding of justice and equity that silenced every angry accusation.

I've experienced moments in my life where I felt the sting of accusations, some stemming from my own mistakes or failures and others sown from the lies of the Enemy. Either way, they all aimed to perpetuate a shame cycle that left me feeling as if I were the problem.

Maybe you can relate. Just remember Jesus never accuses or shames you but points out where he is the most present as he offers himself as the grace-filled answer to every problem you encounter.

## Jesus Valued Women as Equal Heirs

*Then should not this woman, a daughter of Abraham, whom*
*Satan has kept bound for eighteen long years, be set free?*
—Luke 13:16

Only recently did I grasp the depth of the miracle the story of the woman with "a spirit of infirmity" held (Luke 13:11 KJV). Let's dig deeper to uncover the profound layers in this passage. The scene unfolds in a synagogue on a Sabbath, where Jesus was in the middle of teaching when he saw her, a woman who had endured the crippling condition of being bent over for eighteen years (vv. 10–17).

Imagine with me the immense courage it took for her to accept Jesus' invitation and hobble forward, being suddenly thrust into the spotlight. Jesus, moved by compassion, said, "Dear woman, you are healed of your sickness!" Then extending his hand he touched her, and immediately she could stand upright (vv. 13:12–13 NLT).

As with many of his miracles, Jesus was shattering religious constraints. "Indignant because Jesus had healed on the Sabbath, the synagogue leader said to the people, 'There are six days for work. So come and be healed on those days, not on the Sabbath'" (v. 13:14).

Jesus' response was unprecedented: "This dear woman, a *daughter of Abraham*, has been held in bondage by Satan for eighteen years. Isn't it right that she be released, even on the Sabbath?" (v. 13:16 NLT). Jesus reminded the synagogue leaders that they didn't hesitate to free their oxen or donkeys from their stalls to drink water on the Sabbath, emphasizing how much more this woman, bound for eighteen years, deserved to be set free.

She would no longer be known as the crippled woman but as *a daughter of Abraham*.

How many times I have read this and overlooked how monumental this was?

Traditionally Jewish men were referred to as the *sons* of Abraham, but women were never called the *daughters* of Abraham.[11]

In that moment Jesus dismantled age-old biases that devalued women.

When this woman stood upright that day, Jesus did more than heal her. He renamed her, conveying that she had value and as much of a claim to her Jewish heritage as any Jewish man.[12] Jesus communicated her value—not just any kind of value but that of an equal heir to and beneficiary of the promises of Abraham!

This moment holds immense significance because it marked the inclusion of both men and women as sons and daughters in this newly formed people of God, represented and gathered by Jesus himself.

*How beautiful that Jesus saw her and sees you.* Whether you feel unseen, crippled by shame, or bound by a religious tradition that wants to devalue you, be encouraged right now—Jesus sees you, has paid for your freedom, has named you his daughter, and has granted you access as an heir to all he has promised.

## Jesus Invited Women to Be Disciples

> *"Martha, Martha," the Lord answered, "you*
> *are worried and upset about many things,*
> *but few things are needed—or indeed only*
> *one. Mary has chosen what is better, and*
> *it will not be taken away from her."*
>
> —Luke 10:41–42

In our contemporary Western culture, it may not be obvious that Jesus' teaching and discipling women held any significance. As women, most of us get the privilege of unrestricted access to numerous resources and learning opportunities. Yet in Jesus' day, as noted by Dr. Craig Keener, professor of biblical studies at Asbury Theological Seminary, women faced significant educational barriers, having far fewer opportunities than men.[13] One estimate suggests that only one woman out of every five or six men was fully literate.[14]

Although much of the formal religious culture reflected this influence, Jesus engaged in meaningful, intelligent, and deeply spiritual conversations with women, underscoring the significance he placed on all humanity in his kingdom culture.

Let's unearth two striking examples found in the stories of Mary and Martha.

You've likely encountered this first story, but let's not underestimate its remarkable importance. While we often emphasize the contrast between serving and spending time with Jesus, there's a deeper layer to explore. The story revolves around two sisters: Martha, whose role of serving was typical for a woman in that era, and Mary, who sat at Jesus' feet (Luke 10:39).

Perhaps you didn't realize that women didn't sit at the feet of a rabbi; only men did. It's not just Mary's proximity to Rabbi Jesus that's important but her posture; sitting at his feet signified she was his disciple.[15] Not only was Mary neglecting the typical role of a woman, she also had the posture of a student or a disciple. This was nothing short of a revolutionary act. Dr. Kevin Giles writes that Mary "took the male role, where men sit and listen to guests, women prepare food in the kitchen."[16]

When Martha requested that Mary come assist her and stop learning at Jesus' feet as a disciple, Jesus replied, "Mary has chosen what is better, and *it will not be taken away from her*" (v. 10:42). Aída Besançon Spencer, professor of New Testament studies at Gordon-Conwell Theological Seminary, writes that these words take on a deeper meaning when we consider how Jesus "has completely reversed the priorities and the consequences of those priorities in Jewish ancient life. Not only does Jesus *not* think women are exempt from learning the Torah, but also they do *best* to learn God's law ... and [he] will not allow anyone to take this learning process away from those who sit under his feet!"[17] Women had some knowledge of the Torah to manage Shabbat dinners, prepare kosher meals and Passover festivals, or adhere to menstrual purity laws, but Jesus highlighted the importance of their learning theological truth alongside their household responsibilities.

In a culture that considered women intellectually and morally inferior to men, Jesus consistently respected women's capacity to grasp deep intellectual and spiritual truths by including them as his disciples.[18] Rabbis taught male disciples exclusively, so Jesus' followers stood out as they were co-ed and came from diverse backgrounds. He pioneered a radical shift in the culture of his day.

The story of Mary and Martha holds even greater significance because it also illustrates what it meant for a woman to follow Jesus as a disciple while embracing her traditional roles. Jesus didn't suggest women neglect their roles; he expanded their roles as disciples.

As women, many of us must juggle our various roles to keep our world running smoothly, and it can be overwhelming. Jesus' words to Martha still echo over us: "You are worried and distracted by many things.... Mary has chosen the better part" (vv. 10:41–42 CEB).

For us, it's not a question of whether we are Martha or Mary.

We are both.

What a beautiful reminder to every woman who can relate to Martha *and* Mary—while both roles are entrusted, don't forget sitting at his feet first will fuel the rest.

## Martha Wasn't Always Distracted

*Yes, Lord, ... I believe that you are the Messiah,*
*the Son of God, who is to come into the world.*

—John 11:27

Perhaps like me, you may have misunderstood Martha's character, assuming she remained perpetually frustrated and distracted. Though often overlooked, she had one of the most theologically significant conversations with Jesus. In a moment of immense grief, when Martha and Jesus were grappling with the pain of Lazarus's death, Martha's insight and faith were remarkable when she confessed to Jesus, "But I know that even now God will give you whatever you ask" (John 11:22). In a beautiful exchange about death and resurrection, Jesus shared a key insight *first* with Martha: "I am the resurrection and the life. The one who believes in me will live, even though they die; and whoever lives by believing in me will never die" (vv. 11:25–26).

Jesus didn't give this central tenet of our faith to any of the Twelve but to a woman.

Once more, we encounter another *woman* entrusted with the revelation of resurrection. From this interaction with Jesus, it appears that Martha was also deeply committed to learning and being taught, as evidenced in her astute insights into the resurrection—a topic that sparked considerable theological debate within Judaism at the time.

As was customary for rabbis with their disciples, Jesus didn't merely impart truth to her. He activated her mind by asking for her input: "Do you believe this?" (v. 11:26). Remarkably again before they moved the stone from Lazarus's grave, he asked her, "Did I not tell you that if you believe, you will see the glory of God?" (v. 40).

In this tender moment, Martha replied with the same divinely inspired response that Peter gave right before Jesus predicted his death, stating, "I believe that you are the Messiah, the Son of God, who is to come into the world" (John 11:27; for Peter's replies, see Matt. 16:13–20).

Jesus' response to Peter was that *this* confession was the foundation he would build his church on (Matt. 16:13–20). It's remarkable that this God-given theological truth was not only understood but declared by two of Jesus' disciples: Peter, a man, and Martha, a woman. Jesus consistently set a new standard by including men and women as disciples in his kingdom culture, a pattern the early church would follow as well (see chapters 6–7).

As you grasp the worth Jesus assigns to you as an intelligent woman who can comprehend and speak truth, is the "Go tell" echo from him getting louder? I hope so, because you can speak resurrection only when you've experienced it as his disciple by sitting at his feet. This daily practice of cultivating intimacy with Jesus and learning what he says about you will empower you to carry all he's entrusted to you as you influence others.

## Jesus Had Long Conversations with Women

*Many of the Samaritans from that town believed
in him because of the woman's testimony.*
—John 4:39

Although you might recognize this story from John's gospel, its immense but often hidden truth is extraordinary. Let's begin to uncover the layers of this narrative that may have concealed just how valued women are by Jesus.

While the disciples ventured into town to secure dinner, Jesus engaged in a conversation with a Samaritan woman at a well. The story is often told that the woman was alone at the well and shrouded in shame, seeking to avoid judgment from others due to her tainted past. New Testament scholar and author Dr. Lynn Cohick writes there are several clues in the text that "support the view that John's Gospel does not condemn her as an immoral sinner but highlights her as a seeker of truth."[19] Jesus didn't label her as a sinful woman; he spoke to her identity as one who was theologically inquisitive. Nevertheless, under the noonday sun, Jesus embarked on one of the longest and most insightful conversations in the Gospels. The woman posed challenging theological questions, and Jesus attentively addressed her inquiries, never overpowering the conversation or belittling her. As they discussed her life, thirst, and worship, Jesus also unveiled his identity as the Messiah (John 4:25–26). The choice of a woman as the first recipient of this revelation over his male disciples is stunning. It underscores how he involved women and demonstrates his respect for their intellect and his desire for both men *and* women to comprehend truth.

But perhaps even more astounding is that she became the *first female evangelist* (vv. 28–29, 39–42). Her life, wrapped in the pain of five failed marriages—whether divorced or widowed—underwent a profound transformation after she was seen and heard by this Rabbi. She now boldly declared, "Come, see a man who told me everything I ever did" (John 4:29).

This extraordinary story continues, "Many of the Samaritans from that town believed in him because of the *woman's testimony*" (v. 39).

Wait a minute.

Don't miss this, friend.

Not once did Jesus tell her to be quiet because she was a woman. He took the time to disciple her, knowing she had the capacity to understand the truth *and* share it.

Jesus knows your capacity to understand truth and to share it. Don't let the pain of the past silence your story as long as I did. And become inquisitive to learn the truth, like the woman at the well did. Invite God into your story, and watch how he reframes your past and uses it to impact others. If he can use a Samaritan woman's testimony to impact her world, he can use you.

## A Little Change Can Change Everything

> *And it came to pass afterward, that he went throughout every city and village, preaching and shewing the glad tidings of the kingdom of God: and the twelve were with him, and certain women, which had been healed of evil spirits and infirmities, Mary called Magdalene, out of whom went seven devils, and Joanna the wife of Chuza Herod's steward, and Susanna, and many others, which ministered unto him of their substance.*
>
> —Luke 8:1–3 KJV

For years I overlooked the fact that these women were not mere "extras" standing alongside the twelve disciples. I missed the significance of the phrases "and certain women" and "many others," thinking of these women as minor additions to the main story.

But they held immense significance to Jesus' story and ours.

Each of these women had their lives profoundly transformed by Jesus, and as his disciples, they played such a critical role that they are mentioned by name.

Let's dust off the original language to go a little deeper and get a better interpretation of this verse. The word used to describe these women as *ministering* is in fact the same word used to describe the seven men in Acts 6:1–6 as deacons. This word is the Greek verb *diakoneo*, meaning "to serve or minister."[20] However, examining the original language, there is no distinction between the men who ministered (*diakoneo*) and the women who ministered (*diakoneo*), so if the verb appropriately applies to one group, why not the other?

For centuries this one little word has been misinterpreted, but a little change can change a lot.

Both men and women were referred to as ministers who actively and practically served Jesus as his benefactors with their own financial resources, and both testified to the resurrection. Perhaps it's time to consider there was no gender-based distinction in the Greek when it comes to the terms used for men or women leading, ministering, and serving together. Michael Wilkins sums it up best: "Jesus restored and affirmed women to his ministry team, as co-laborers with men."[21]

## The Twelve Male Apostles

> *When morning came, he called his*
> *disciples to him and chose twelve of them,*
> *whom he also designated apostles.*
>
> —Luke 6:13

Some scholars argue that the pattern of the twelve Jewish male disciples is a clear example of excluding women from leadership roles. However, New Testament scholar Philip Payne contends that Jesus' "choice of the twelve apostles does not logically exclude women from church leadership any more than his choice of free Jews for the twelve apostles excludes gentiles ... from church leadership."[22] He highlights that James and Paul, not part of the original Twelve, are still considered apostles, just like Junia, a woman whom Paul described as "outstanding among the apostles" (Rom. 16:7).[23] Some scholars suggest the twelve apostles symbolize the twelve tribes and represent the restoration of the "new Israel."[24] Maybe it's time to reconsider the traditional depiction of the Twelve plus Jesus as indicating only men can lead in the church. Additionally, the representation of the Twelve fades into the early church's landscape, and the evidence we've just seen of Jesus including women in his ministry invites a fresh consideration of this long-standing perspective that God limited discipleship and apostleship to only men.

## At the Cross and Resurrection

*There were also women watching from a distance. Among them were Mary Magdalene, Mary the mother of James the younger and of Joses, and Salome. In Galilee these women followed him and took care of him.* Many other women *had come up with him to Jerusalem.*

—Mark 15:40–41 CSB

Imagine with me what a beautiful picture this was: Jesus on his last trip into Jerusalem surrounded by his disciples as he was about to face the cross. Beautiful—yet rare and unheard of—because of the substantial presence of female disciples with male disciples. This wasn't the norm; rabbis didn't travel with female disciples. These women, many with families and homes, had all been transformed and discipled by his ministry and were as much a part of his ministry as the men.

While the start of Jesus' earthly ministry was characterized by the calling of Peter, Andrew, John, and James to follow him,[25] in the passion story, only John and the three female disciples, Mary, Salome, and Mary,[26] were present at the cross. As many of the disciples retreated in fear, these women were not only present to hear Jesus' final words—"It is finished" (John 19:30)—but a woman was the first to hear the words of a resurrected Savior. And the first to be entrusted with telling others of his resurrection. How can we downplay the importance of women in the gospel story when they played such a significant role in serving Jesus until the very end?

## Proclaiming the Good News

Jesus didn't let the cultural narrative stop him from giving a woman the responsibility of testifying to what all of humanity and heaven had been waiting to hear.

The resurrection.

Consider what Jesus did for women:

> He included them in his story.
> He brought them into his inner circle.
> He honored their intelligence to handle even the
>     deepest truths.
> He invited them into discipleship.

He called them daughters of Abraham.

He trusted their testimony even when the legal courts didn't.

He encouraged them to use their voices with the culmination of the gospel story by commissioning a woman to announce his resurrection to her "brothers."

If Jesus consistently treated women as equal to men, then I must assume any theology of women that does not treat them equally is not in line with the principles Jesus lived.

So, what am I saying?

I'm saying this: Jesus made it abundantly clear that he could not accept biases that denied his daughters the same entrustment as his sons within his kingdom.

Even the Protestant Reformer John Calvin (1509–1564) noted that while the disciples didn't believe the women at first, "when they afterwards proclaimed the gospel, they must have borrowed from women the chief portion of the history."[27]

Jesus chose a woman's voice as the primary account of the resurrection narrative.

Because of Mary Magdalene's testimony we, as women and men, have a story to tell.

Jesus commissioned Mary and you, as women, to serve alongside men to build the church.

Jesus not only overcame death, hell, and the grave; he also put the good news of the resurrection in *your* mouth.

Mary became the first among many women to proclaim the good news, and it marked the beginning of the prophetic fulfillment of this beautiful messianic promise in Psalm 68:11: "The women who proclaim the good news are a great host" (AMP).

And you and I and the generations of women to come are a part of that great host!

## The Evidence in Your Life

Do you feel a bit covered in dust after that excavation of the Gospels? Or has it cleaned the lens through which you see Jesus, making it clear how he cherishes you?

I couldn't wait for you to discover how accounts of women serving alongside men are richly woven throughout the gospel story. Whether this has left you in awe or you're sensing tension, I want to encourage you to keep digging for yourself. Remember, my goal is to spark your curiosity, as A. W. Tozer wrote, to take an "intelligent and vigorous" look at the Bible.

My hope is that the echo of how Jesus treated women becomes louder to you, friend.

That the question Jesus asked Mary—"Who are you looking for?"—is like a GPS device, inviting you to pay attention to where your thoughts and mindset have brought you.

That you can shake off the pain and fear that has kept you hiding the entrustment.

And that you, my friend, hear the echo over your life of how valued and esteemed you are by the One who sees where you are right now at this moment in your life. That you see him as your dearly loved Rabbi who is passionately pursuing you and speaking to you as his *disciple*.

May you be covered with the dust of your Rabbi as you closely follow him, the One who loves, sees, and values you the most.

Next, we're going to look at the origin of that garden echo; it's going to blow your mind ...

Get ready.

## Hineni

*Lord, here I am. Thank you for esteeming, valuing, and including me in your story, for reframing my shame and pain into a way that testifies to you.*

Take a moment to personalize your hineni prayer of surrender. In what areas has God entrusted you to echo his resurrection? What fresh commitment do you need to make?

...............................................................................................................

...............................................................................................................

...............................................................................................................

...............................................................................................................

...............................................................................................................

...............................................................................................................

...............................................................................................................

...............................................................................................................

*I say yes to all you have for me. Hineni.*

# Chapter 5

# The Original Trust

*Life is a sum of all your choices.*
—Albert Camus

Should I work out today or hit the snooze button?

Should I buy the shoes at full price or wait for the sale?

Should I eat carrots or chips and salsa? (Personally, I'd go with chips and salsa every time.)

Every day our brain navigates through an estimated thirty-five thousand choices, from the small, seemingly inconsequential to the big, life-changing decisions, whether it's choosing what to eat for breakfast, finding the right job, or deciding whom to marry.[1] This might explain why many of us experience decision fatigue, given the staggering volume of choices we make daily!

The intricate process of making a choice involves various regions of your brain: the prefrontal cortex, which handles planning and decision-making, and the amygdala, which manages emotions and assesses potential risks and rewards, both of which influence what you choose.[2] At this very moment, your synapses are firing based on what you choose to believe as you read the words on these pages.

Maybe, like myself, you are astounded at this revelation about how those daily decisions activate your brain. Indeed, grasping the significance of our daily choices is crucial as they play a pivotal role in shaping our future.

And this revelation goes all the way back to the beginning, to the first garden, where a single choice reverberated throughout time and affected all of us. I want to activate your brain as we dig into the echo from Jesus' lips that came from the "original trust" in Genesis.

> I will make your pains in childbearing very severe;
>> with painful labor you will give birth to children.
> Your desire will be for your husband,
>> and he will rule over you. (Gen. 3:16)

Ouch!

These words were part of God's message to Eve after she and Adam betrayed his trust in the garden of Eden. Pain. Childbearing. More pain. And, oh yeah, your husband will rule over you. Perhaps even the most humorless among us can chuckle a little at the idea of a husband being a sort of climactic punishment. And yet, for centuries Christians have used this and other verses in the creation story to support their belief that God has limited women's value, purpose, and authority and keeps women on the sidelines.

We've seen already that Jesus loved, called, and empowered women and men together. So how can we make sense of this passage since it seems to contradict what we just read in the last chapter? Can you sense the tension and confusion it presents? Good, I hope you can. Instead of ignoring that tension, let's jump right into it and see if there's any way to reconcile it.

Perhaps, like me, you didn't initially see the significance of exploring the original language or context of Genesis 1–3. Yet we can't read the creation story at a surface level—with today's language and context—and absorb its depth of meaning. These passages hold gems for us from the original trust given to us by our heavenly Father. Increased access to the original languages and documents has expanded scholars' understanding, improving our knowledge of what God communicates to both men and women. My hope as you read is that you'll see God's intention in our origin story because it is significant for *your* story.

Imagine: You inherit great wealth from your grandfather, secured in a trust in a safe-deposit box. Decades pass, yet you remain unaware of the accessible riches available to you, leaving the box unopened.

Similarly, God, your Father, has stored treasures for you to uncover in his story. Yet, too often they remain undiscovered, as you are unaware of what you've been entrusted to steward. Only by reading the original trust do you find the full inheritance you've somehow missed.

To understand the original trust in Genesis 3, let's go back to the beginning. I believe you'll see that Jesus' call to women both redeemed and echoed the origin story of the first woman. We'll also discover that the *choice*—between entrusted or entitled—is a significant part of the story and was there from the start.

## The Curtain Opens

*And the LORD God planted a garden eastward in Eden; and there he put the man whom he had formed. And out of the*

*ground made the LORD God to grow every tree that is pleasant*
*to the sight, and good for food; the tree of life also in the midst*
*of the garden, and the tree of knowledge of good and evil.*

—Genesis 2:8–9 KJV

As a child, I often pictured the setting of this story as a lush garden filled with the most delightful greenery and woven with the full spectrum of color and every type of flower and fruit.

Hold up.

Do me a favor. Pause right now and grab your Bible. Read the first three chapters of Genesis. Or Google them. You need this background.

In the first five days of creation, everything that came into existence was preceded by "And God said ..." (Gen. 1). The world as we know it came into existence from nothing. From the boundary lines God placed on darkness when he said, "Let there be light" (1:3), to the lush green of the garden teeming with life and animals to bodies of land and water ... all of it from God's spoken word.

Take a second to marvel at the power of God's voice setting into motion creation that is still teeming with the life he spoke. Every word filled with the seeds of endless possibilities within it to reproduce. What you see outside your window is a direct result of the words God spoke. Indeed, the weight of his words still moves mountains and works miracles today!

God's words carry the profound ability to transform how you see whatever challenges you're facing right now. The Bible is the only book in which the Author is passionately in love with the reader. The words brim with the very essence of the Author who breathes life into you as you read.

The artist Makoto Fujimura writes, "The Genesis account is not just about the idea of Creation, but about the actual process of the Incarnation, of God's love to create the universe."[3] Consider the stunning picture of God's love story for his masterpiece (Eph. 2:10). Reflecting on God's care in crafting Adam and Eve in his image reveals the depth of his love. The sheer level of trust and authority given to the first two humans as co-regents to steward their entrustment was truly remarkable.

Reading God's story through a lens of entrustment versus one of entitlement opens our eyes to the vast difference in posture that all of humanity wrestles with.

It was just one subtle lie: that if Adam and Eve ate from the one tree God was "holding back" from them, they would be like him.

Wait, weren't they already like him?

And herein lies the battle.

The battle that keeps us from seeing what we've *already* been entrusted with.

We have all been made in God's image, and the subtlety of a scarcity mentality—seeing things through a lens of what we lack—always opens the door to entitlement. *If only I had more _____, then I would be more likely to succeed, or have more, or be more.*

When entitlement jumps into the story and becomes the narrator, we lose our identity and our authority ... and, more importantly, our intimacy with our Creator.

But don't take my word for it. Let's dive deep into what this means for humanity.

Not only do I want you to grasp what Jesus thinks about you, but I want you to see that when he appeared to the woman in the second garden, he was redeeming what was lost in the first garden.

Perhaps the heart of the creation story revolves around the entrustment God gave to men and women and the power of choice.

## Entrusted with His Image

*Then God said, "Let us make mankind in our image, in our likeness, so that they may rule over the fish in the sea and the birds in the sky, over the livestock and all the wild animals, and over all the creatures that move along the ground."*

*So God created mankind in his own image, in the image of God he created them; male and female he created them.*

—Genesis 1:26–27

Our self-image significantly impacts how we live, shaping our stories. Our unique experiences mark us, and the resulting labels we adopt often define how we see ourselves. Too often for women, the pervasive notion that we're weaker overshadows every aspect of our story. For years, I wore the label of victim due to abuse, which, in turn, limited my ability to understand my purpose to be a leader of change. Perhaps you've been wearing a label God didn't give you, one that was shaped by a lie.

So, is "weaker" the label God assigns to us, and if not, where did it originate?

Throughout church history, many scholars[4] maintained that the order of creation in Genesis signified man's superiority because men were created in God's image first and then women in the image of man.[5] Because of the order of creation, Eve was often regarded as having lesser value than Adam, and she was blamed for the fall. Consequently, women throughout history were unfairly labeled as the weaker half of humanity intellectually, emotionally, spiritually, and morally.

I find this perspective based on the order of creation puzzling because if you follow it, plant and animal life were created *before* man, suggesting they would have greater value and authority than humans. As much as our grand-dogs, Lola and Remi, would like to think they're in charge, we know this can't be right!

Perhaps the order of creation in the Genesis narrative highlights individual worth and mutual dependence.[6]

The initial five days of creation were preceded by the words "God said"; however, a profound shift happens with the words, "Let us make humanity in our image" (Gen. 1:26 CEB). This signals a deeper intimacy as God personally shaped both male and female by breathing life into them; the very essence of who he is, setting them apart from the rest of creation.

Now, let's dig into the trust you've been given. Do you have your pen out? I want you to take some notes, because grasping the concept that men and women were created in the *imago Dei* is incredibly powerful.

The significance of the Hebrew word for "image"—*tselem*—being repeated three times in these few verses (vv. 26–27) shouldn't be ignored. It's kind of like when you were a kid and your mom called your name three times—you knew it wasn't the moment to pretend you didn't hear!

When God repeats himself several times, he wants to make sure we don't miss it.

So then, what does it mean to be created in the image of God?

Sandra Richter in *The Epic of Eden* writes about the specific implications of the word *tselem* for ancient Near Eastern cultures. When we merge the language of Genesis 1:26–27 with the imagery of Genesis 2:7, Yahweh reveals himself as a divine craftsman, creating an image of himself that he must animate—and that image is us. Richter explains that "within the worldview of the ancient Near East the message here is clear: we are the nearest representation of Yahweh that exists."[7]

Did you catch that? We are the nearest representation of God! And when God assessed his masterpiece, he didn't settle for "good," but declared humans "very good" (v. 1:31). He considered us bearers of his likeness with extraordinary worth.

Mind-blowing, isn't it?

Additionally, it was common in practice in the ancient Near East to erect an image of the deity worshipped in a specific territory to serve as a substitute for the divine presence.[8]

Astonishingly, instead of a stone image of himself, God created us. This is why God prohibited Israel from crafting stone images of him, because he had already molded his image *within* us![9]

Richter emphasizes that the aspects that most mirror the *imago Dei* are captured in the phrase "Let us," which signifies both male and female in relationship, reflecting the relationship of the original,[10] representing the Father, Son, and Holy Spirit as a community. In essence, the image we bear together as man and woman is to reflect the same oneness of relationship that the Father, Son, and Holy Spirit share.[11] One gender doesn't carry a higher value or closer resemblance to God than the other![12]

This means the entrusted image of God is both male and female functioning together.

We carry the image of God everywhere we go as we represent him on the earth.

In fact, Paul continued this thought when he wrote that we "have put on the new self, which is being renewed in knowledge in the image of its Creator" (Col. 3:10). The more we discover God, the more we can reflect his image and the more we find those old labels don't fit us anymore.

Go ahead. Begin discarding any labels that suggest you're the weaker side of humanity or that tell you anything different from what God says about who you are. Women and men "are necessary as equal partners reflecting the image of God."[13]

But keep reading; bearing his image isn't the only entrustment. Let's explore what God calls you.

## Entrusted as a Helper

> *The LORD God said, "It is not good for the man to*
> *be alone. I will make a* helper *suitable for him."*
> —Genesis 2:18

Now that you've got the entrustment of the image of God down a bit more, I want you to fully grasp the first name God gives women that holds profound purpose for you. Perhaps you've missed it for years as I did, but understanding this is crucial.

While we reflect the image of God together with men, the first name God calls women adds deeper significance to our purpose.

God calls us a *helper*.

In the Hebrew, the word is *ezer*, and the full definition is astounding.

*Ezer* appears twenty-one times in the Hebrew Scriptures, translated various ways but always implying one who offers assistance, empowers others, is a capable and strong ally, or serves another with what is needed.[14] It is used twice to reference a woman[15] and sixteen times in reference to God himself as the helper.[16]

While the English term *helper* is often used to refer to someone who is inferior, we would never consider God as *ezer* in this light. So, have we perhaps missed the true meaning of *helper*?

## A Capable, Powerful, and Intelligent Ally

Genesis tells us that after Adam named all the animals, a problem still existed: "But for Adam there was not found a helper *comparable* [*ezer kenegdo*] to him" (2:20 NKJV). The words *ezer kenegdo* "describe the person who would satisfy what was missing in the man's life: a companion ... like himself."[17]

The depth of meaning for *ezer* is even more beautiful when combined with the word *kenegdo* in this verse.

God used the word *comparable* or *suitable* to describe the woman as a solution to the man's problem. This word in the Hebrew, *kenegdo*, appears only once in the Bible, and it means more than just a person who shares similar interests.

"The phrase *kenegdo* is best translated as 'corresponding to him,' a term that implies competence and equality, rather than subordination or inferiority."[18] An equal counterpart[19] with a strength, might, or valor equivalent to him, one who was on equal footing.[20] "Woman was not intended to be merely man's helper. She was to be instead his partner,"[21] an intelligent ally.

So when putting these two words together, a *suitable helper* is far more than one who bakes a cake while Adam names the animals. (Not to devalue your baking ability—that's a highly respected gift I lack!)

In other words, the woman was equally capable of carrying out the creation mandate entrusted to both the man and the woman as partners and co-regents.

In case you missed this, as a woman, the name that God calls you—*ezer kenegdo*—is one of strength. The creation account offers a beautiful picture of men and women partnering together in their unique God-given gifts—equal in essence and role—to accomplish the mission God entrusted to humanity. In fact, I think we could say that men and women were created to be on the #sameteam.

When I need help beyond my abilities, I find someone skilled and capable. Whether it's parenting dilemmas, relational drama, financial issues, or leadership issues, I turn to someone who is capable of helping me. Someone who enhances what I lack and brings solutions to my need and purpose.

I look for an *ezer*.

So, friends, when God calls you an *ezer*, he sees your potential, what you already possess, and the areas in which you will continue to grow as you lean on your Creator and *Ezer* to help you. You serve as an intelligent ally, strong, capable, and able to come alongside and empower others by serving them.

And you stand in good company with other *ezers* throughout the Old Testament who shaped history with the men they served alongside—Deborah, Ruth, Esther, Rahab, Huldah, Hannah, Abigail, just to name a few who were all on the #sameteam.

Generations of *ezers* have pioneered the path before you. Many of them are unknown, but their yes shaped history, giving us a foundation to stand on.

*You* are part of this company of *ezers*—co-regents, strong allies, partners alongside men—as we steward together the unique entrustment God has given us at this moment in history to build his kingdom.

God's perfect story for humanity, like every compelling tale, has an antagonist attempting to sabotage the narrative. Will our story end with the fruit of an entrusted garden of possibilities or a graveyard of lost potential?

Our story hinges on our choices.

## Entrusted with Stewardship and the Power of Choice

> *Then God blessed* them, *and God said to them, "Be*
> *fruitful and multiply; fill the earth and subdue it; have*
> *dominion over the fish of the sea, over the birds of the air,*
> *and over every living thing that moves on the earth."*
>
> —Genesis 1:28 NKJV

Adam and Eve, as image bearers representing God's presence on the earth, were given the role to function as stewards together. Genesis 1:28 clearly states "God blessed *them*" as they stood shoulder to shoulder,[22] with equal authority and dominion.

Doesn't it sound like how we have already defined *leadership*?

It's not our authority we are stewarding but the authority we've been granted by God.

I want to highlight the connection between God not only granting Adam and Eve authority and dominion but *also* prohibiting them from eating from a specific tree (v. 2:17).

You may not realize this, but the prohibition was an empowerment from God for Adam and Eve by giving them the *power of choice*.

> ## Will our story end with the fruit of an entrusted garden of possibilities or a graveyard of lost potential?

Grasping this fundamental truth is crucial to effective leadership.

Rather than viewing God's restraints as *obstacles* to your purpose, recognize that every entrustment contains a *choice*.

What Adam and Eve chose to do regarding their entrustment would define their identity, authority, and relationship, just as your choices do for you.

If you honor God's authority and entrustment, he'll give you the entire garden.

So, Adam and Eve were given the power of choice to partake of all the trees in the garden *except* the tree of knowledge of good and evil (vv. 16–17). This choice to obey or not obey was, at its foundation, their decision to make.

It's one we all must make.

To decide to remain dependent or independent.

The choice to pick a different sovereign.

*Wait, what do you mean? God was their sovereign, right?*

Yes, but Adam and Eve were given the freedom to choose if they wanted to serve God as their sovereign, the One who created them for intimacy and relationship, the One who gave them everything they could possibly need or want.

Did they want the world God gave them or one of their own choosing?

The one *entrusted* to them or the one they felt *entitled* to?

Did they want to be dependent on God as their sovereign or independent by being their own sovereign? Humanity's perfect world by God's design rested on the power of choice.

Sandra Richter writes, "Did *'Ādām* [Adam and Eve] want this world? Or one of their making? The ones made in the image of God could not be forced or coerced, but instead were called upon to *choose* their sovereign."[23]

Sheesh ...

So, although they were handed the *trust*, they had to decide to follow the instructions or choose their own way of doing it.

The power of persuasion[24] by the serpent when he posed the question "Did God really say, 'You can't eat from any tree in the garden'?" (Gen. 3:1 CSB) caused Eve to begin to question the *goodness* of God. The serpent led her to believe that God was holding back the best, that if she and Adam ate from the forbidden tree, they would be "more than" they already were.

Their eyes would be opened, and they would be like God.

The original trust of the *imago Dei* and their co-regency were put in the balances by the battle over entrustment and entitlement.

For in yielding to the desire to see and be more by eating the fruit of the one tree they were prohibited from, Eve missed seeing the entire entrustment of a lush garden filled with more than enough.

You see, living and leading with the authority you've been given always involves a choice. We get to choose daily: to see what we've already been *entrusted* with or yield to the lie of the Enemy that tells us God is somehow holding back goodness we are *entitled* to.

Indeed, all of us deal with this battle daily; it's part of being human.

And our daily choices determine the future we live.

## Fallen Women and Fallen Men in a Fallen World

Let's look at Eve's reply to the serpent because it was a distortion of God's actual words as she claimed that God had said, "You must not touch it [the fruit]" (Gen. 3:3).

God *actually* said, "You must not eat" it (v. 2:17).

But why does this matter? Because Eve's response to the serpent was a half-truth (a.k.a. a lie). I call it a "half-truth lie" because its danger lies in its initial connection to the truth, which is why we often miss it.

And the story, now laced with a half-truth lie, subtly began to change the way Eve saw God. It sparked doubts of God's goodness, which led her to believe that she and Adam were lacking and not enough because God was withholding something important from them.

If only they had more knowledge, they would be more like God.

They *already* carried his image, right?

Half-truth lies are how the Enemy gets us to shift from entrusted to entitled thinking and lose our identity in the process.

All. The. Time.

You, friend, are bombarded daily with half-truth lies that make you want to give up your unique entrustment and instead chase after entitlement because surely God is withholding something from you.

It's part of life and part of carrying the entrusted influence and leadership God has already given you. It's usually not a rapid shift but a slow one. Little by little, the Enemy persuades us.

It's what happened to Eve. Temptation's persuasion entered with a half-truth lie, shifting her perspective of entrustment to entitlement, forever changing God's original purpose of blessing into sin's curse, and ultimately disrupting our relationship of oneness with our Creator and with one another.

This wasn't the end of the story but an invitation to see how every choice holds the potential for redemption when God is involved.

But let's look at Genesis 3:16 again, which initially felt at odds with how Jesus valued women. Now that we have a deeper understanding of the Genesis narrative, the tension intensifies. Was God indicating perpetual conflict between the genders?

I think Scot McKnight, a New Testament scholar, sums it up best:

> The fall distorted mutuality by turning women against men and men against women; oneness became otherness and rivalry for power. Here are the climactic, tragic words from Genesis 3:16: "Your desire will be for your husband, and he will rule over

you." We read here a prediction of what life will be like for those living in otherness instead of oneness.

The sin of Adam and Eve, or better yet, Eve and Adam, created tension in the relationship. The woman's desire is for the man but the man's desire is corrupted to rule over her. Her sin turned the woman to seek dominance over the man, and the man's sin turned the man to seek dominance over the woman.[25]

Instead of a *prescription*, these two lines are a *prediction* of the fallen desire of fallen women and fallen men in a fallen condition in a fallen world.... The desire to dominate is a broken desire. The redeemed desire is to love in mutuality. This verse in Genesis 3, in other words, predicts a struggle of fallen wills; they don't prescribe how we are *supposed* to live.[26]

Humanity needed a redeemer.

It is important to see that God's intention of equality for his creation did not change; instead, embedded in the curse is the tragic result of human sin. Authors and scholars Derek and Dianne Tidball write, "Eve and Adam's disobedience throws the compass that had indicated the direction God intended human beings to follow out of alignment."[27]

Jesus is the redeemer we all needed. His sacrificial love and death on the cross paid the full price for our sin, set us free from the curse, and reset the compass (Gal. 3:13–14).

The good news is that the Bible from beginning to end is the story of how God's love redeems a broken humanity, leading to a new creation through Christ (Gal. 3:28; 2 Cor. 5:17), one that is marked by servant leadership rather than dominance.

From the first garden to the second, the entrustment remains the same. Men and women have been given the *imago Dei* as co-regents and allies (not adversaries!) to build and steward the kingdom *together* here on the earth so humanity can flourish in God's promises.

I'm excited for you to discover in the next chapter how God's entrustment to both genders is a beautiful redemptive thread woven into the fabric of the New Testament church.

But remember this: You, my friend, have been named an *ezer* by your Creator, God. And we stand in good company with generations of *ezers* who pioneered at great personal cost for us to stand where we do today.

All of us get to eat the fruit from the garden their obedience planted.

From the first garden to the second, God's entrustment to you is a beautiful story. I hope you take off any false labels, ones that God didn't give you. Become aware of those half-truth lies that tell you that you're not enough, and lean into all God has for you.

You have been entrusted with his image to represent him right where you are.

Let's consider God's first question to Adam and Eve—"Where are you?" (Gen. 3:9)—as a starting point for reflection; as with any journey, when using a GPS, knowing your starting point is crucial.

Remove any labels God didn't give you, and embrace the name he calls you: *ezer*, a strong, intelligent ally who's been entrusted to steward your God-given gifts.

You never know the generations that will be affected by your yes.

## Hineni

*Lord, here I am. I say yes to the entrustment redeemed by Jesus from the original trust, and I surrender the labels that have defined me that didn't come from you. I commit to be the* ezer *you've called me to be.*

Take a moment to personalize your hineni prayer of surrender. What labels have you picked up that are keeping you from seeing yourself as the *ezer* God called you to be? What fresh commitment do you need to make?

.................................................................................................

.................................................................................................

.................................................................................................

.................................................................................................

.................................................................................................

.................................................................................................

.................................................................................................

.................................................................................................

*I say yes to all you have for me. Hineni.*

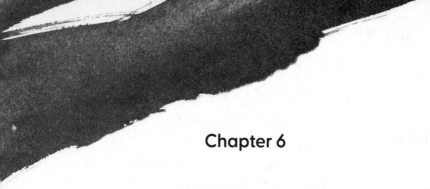

# Chapter 6

# Flipping Tables

*If I have seen further, it is by standing
on the shoulders of giants.*

—Sir Isaac Newton

I am directionally challenged.

I was born this way. Unlike my forefathers who navigated oceans by merely looking at the sky for direction, sadly, this gift was not passed down to me through the generations. I *still* have a difficult time using the navigational app on my phone to assess the distance of 0.06 miles to the next exit and either drive too far with my blinker on or miss the exit entirely!

Whether you are like me or you are the gifted one everyone leans on during a road trip, each of us at some point has struggled with navigating the most contentious verses from Paul's letters concerning women's roles.

Hindered by a lack of understanding the road map laid out for us in the Bible, many of us struggle in our journey to discover the purpose and the gifts entrusted to us. Unfortunately, we can miss the destination God is calling us to because it's been hidden for so long.

Regardless of where you are on your journey, whether you're deeply involved in ministry or navigating where to start, this chapter aims to provide greater clarity to you in discovering your place in God's story.

Before we continue, let me just warn you … the tension you may feel around these next two chapters is real. And so is the confusion.

Paul's writings have been used to silence women for centuries, as people built entire doctrines around a few verses while missing context and the author's intent. As we navigate the original language and the first-century Jewish context, we'll discover Paul's words weren't meant to be a "lid" on women leading or speaking as some suggest. Rather, we'll explore how Paul's influence on the early church echoes Jesus' intent for women and aligns with God's mandate in Genesis for both genders. This one cohesive story is seen in the first sermon on the day of Pentecost, when the church was birthed, where both genders were empowered.

Paul literally flipped the table on the culture!

A few things to remember before you pick up your pen to take notes. I am not trying to persuade you what to believe but rather to spark your curiosity for your own exploration. The theology we believe is for confidence, not combat. In other words, our theology was never meant to be weaponized but to stir a theological humility by staying curious as we study the text.

The tone we hear when we read something is crucial and is often filtered through our experiences and knowledge.

We've all had the annoying experience of sending a text to someone who becomes offended because they've assumed a tone that wasn't our intention.

My mama used to wisely tell me: "People can't hear the intention of what you're saying if they misread your tone."

You quickly learn that tone and context matter.

I wonder if we've been reading Paul's letters through a tone that is limiting rather than permission giving.

Imagine this scenario: As I gaze out the window one day, I turn to my husband and say "Let's spend the day relaxing" with no more details than that. He agrees, assuming we will spend the day at a pickleball court while I'm envisioning the beach. When we converge at the front door, our surprise becomes evident. He's sporting pickleball shorts while I'm in my bathing suit and sandals. We both want relaxation, but different filters have led us to envision different destinations.

If a picture is worth a thousand words, then context is worth a million! And as we've learned so far, it's essential we don't ignore the tension in the text but instead sit in it and wrestle with tone and context to discover truth.

As we read God's story, we must read it holistically. We can't take one verse out of context. We must read the descriptive, instructive, and corrective verses together to determine a deeper meaning. Put simply, it's essential to first examine the verses where Paul *described* the roles of the women he served with before diving into any verses that *instruct* or *correct*.

## Every Significant Name

Read the following two sentences out loud right now, and then raise your hand for the one that hits closest to home:

"I'm giving up eating chocolate for a month."

"I'm giving up. Eating chocolate for a month."

I've probably felt *both* running unchecked through my brain just in the last forty-eight hours while writing this book. This is a simple example of how context, punctuation, and experience affect meaning.

Did you know that the numbered chapters and verses we use as reference points in the Bible weren't even incorporated into the actual text until an edition of the Latin Vulgate was printed in 1551?[1] Too often, a verse number or chapter break results in a disconnected thought that wasn't separated in the original document.

For example, you've probably quoted Philippians 4:13 at some point in your life when facing a battle or insurmountable obstacle. As long as we have God on our side, we can do anything, tackle our to-do list, or accomplish that massive goal. But defining it like this is taking it out of context. Here is the entire thought Paul wrote (from the context of prison by the way):

> I have learned to be content whatever the circumstances. I know what it is to be in need, and I know what it is to have plenty. I have learned the secret of being content in any and every situation, whether well fed or hungry, whether living in plenty or in want. I can do all this through him who gives me strength. (vv. 11–13)

While you *can* overcome that obstacle, the root of what Paul was writing was learning to be content by applying God's grace to endure any hardship.

A little different with the full context, right?

Romans 16 is another chapter that for years, I am embarrassed to say, I skimmed over. I've thought, *I don't know these people, so I'll just skip it to get to the good parts.* It seemed to be the least inspiring part of Paul's letter to the church in Rome. But I missed something very important in that list of thank-yous and shout-outs from Paul.

These are the people who partnered with him in ministry.

Every name is significant because every name has a story behind it.

Even more remarkable is that, unless you dive in further, you might overlook that Paul was including names of men *and* women in a leadership capacity.

Wait. A. Second.

Let me say that again because I don't want you to miss this massive point. Perhaps we have missed this for centuries and have been "wearing pickleball shorts to the pool."

The ending of the letter to the Romans expresses Paul's gratitude for those who partnered with him in ministry. Of the twenty-nine people Paul wrote about in the last chapter, *ten are women*!

Hopefully I sparked some curiosity to see who these people were, specifically the women whose shoulders we now stand on two thousand years later.

Go ahead and fasten your seat belt as we navigate this journey to explore Paul's perspective on women with a fresh lens!

## Equal Honor

The apostle Paul wrote in Galatians 3:28, "There is neither Jew nor Gentile, neither slave nor free, nor is there male and female, for you are all one in Christ Jesus." This statement alone was groundbreaking simply because before his conversion, as a rabbi and former pharisee, it is possible that Paul would have greeted each day with this prayer:[2]

> Praise be to you, Adonai our God, King of the universe, who has not made me *a Gentile*. Praise be to You, Adonai our God, King of the universe, who has not made me *a slave*. Praise to You, Adonai, our God, King of the universe, who has not made me *a woman*.[3]

It's possible he prayed like this ... until he had an encounter with Jesus.

It is no accident that Paul would have used the same three groupings—*Jew/Gentile, slave/free, male/female*—in his writing to the newly formed church in Galatia. He knew that Jesus had come to usher in a new creation, one that reflected the original intent in Genesis, the oneness God created for both genders to partner together. Paul shifted a culture of hierarchy to one in which status and titles were irrelevant in Christ.[4] Gordon Fee maintains that in the new creation, ethnicity, status, and gender no longer determine value or social identity.[5] Put simply, these categories hold no sway over the significance of worth, and *equal honor should be extended to both parties*. Paul's statement is a beautiful *descriptive* picture of how he influenced the early church in his leadership.

So then, if Paul *only* corrected and restricted women, it would seem inconsistent and kind of weird, right? Did he change his theology midstream?

Before we explore Paul's instructive and corrective texts in the next chapter, let's focus on the descriptive ones that highlight the women Paul partnered with and felt deserved recognition.

We stand on the shoulders of these women who, at great personal sacrifice, helped build the early church. Since many of these women have been hidden for so long, go ahead and say their names out loud while you're reading.

You stand on *their* shoulders.

## Phoebe

> *I [Paul] commend to you our sister Phoebe, a deacon*
> *of the church in Cenchreae. I ask you to receive her*
> *in the Lord in a way worthy of his people and to give*
> *her any help she may need from you, for she has been*
> *the benefactor of many people, including me.*
>
> —Romans 16:1–2

Perhaps like me, you've missed Phoebe's significance in the early church. From Paul's description of her, we learn that Phoebe served as a minister (deacon), a generous benefactor, and his emissary to Rome. Tradition holds that she delivered Paul's letter to the new church plant in Rome.[6] Talk about navigating a journey! It required courage to travel, not to mention to accomplish the mission Paul had entrusted to her. This seven-hundred-mile trek was dangerous for anyone, especially a woman; Phoebe didn't hop into her Tesla and roll over the hills to Rome. As a courier, Phoebe not only safeguarded the letter but also read it aloud to convey Paul's tone and emphasis. In fact, many scholars believe she may have practiced reading it aloud with Paul.

Furthermore, she was responsible for addressing any theological questions from the six house churches in Rome at the time.[7] This implies she had a thorough understanding of the entire letter written by Paul.

Not only did Paul choose Phoebe as his letter bearer to the Roman church[8] but he also *commended* her! The Greek word for *commend*, "to stand with," reflects his unwavering endorsement of her. In a status-obsessed patriarchal culture, Paul's endorsement of a woman was groundbreaking. Let's not miss the significance of this. Paul entrusted the book of Romans—one of the most theologically comprehensive letters he wrote—to a woman!

Paul understood the significance of his request of Phoebe and wanted to assure the new church plant that he trusted and highly recommended her, emphasizing her credibility as an emissary by the apostle himself.[9]

Here's a second thing we can't miss.

He called her "a deacon," a *diakonos*, the same term Paul used for himself[10] and Apollos in 1 Corinthians 3:5. (Does this term ring a bell? In chapter 4, we looked at a similar Greek verb, *diakoneo*, that was used for the women who followed Jesus.) It is also used in Philippians 1:1 to describe Paul and Timothy and in 1 Timothy 3:8 and 12 when Paul described to Timothy the character traits to look for in church deacons. Each instance refers to church leadership and ministry; therefore, doesn't it make sense the same definition be applied regardless of gender?

A third point is Paul's encouragement to "receive her in the Lord in a *way worthy of his people*" (Rom. 16:2). He anticipated the Roman church would potentially hold a gender bias against her, which could hinder them from embracing Paul's message.

But then Paul gave Phoebe full authority and support like a credit card with no limit, ensuring she had everything necessary to fulfill her responsibilities.

He did this by asking the Roman church to "help," or "stand with," her (v. 2). He was saying as *he* stood with her, he wanted *them* to stand with her for whatever "she may need."

At this point in Phoebe's reading, I'm curious if the Roman listeners in the first century started wondering who this woman really was!

Paul qualified his recommendation and instructions by telling them Phoebe was a "benefactor of many people," including Paul himself (v. 2).

Stay with me, friend, as we venture deeper into the original language for a minute to gain clarity. The Greek word for *benefactor* is *prostatis*, which comes from the verb *proistemi,* which means "to exercise a position of leadership."[11] The word *prostatis* is only used once in the New Testament; though traditionally it is translated as "helper" or "benefactor," a better translation is "leader."[12] This term also implies that Phoebe was independently wealthy and serving as a patron or benefactor who financially supported Paul's ministry. Paul urged Rome to honor and respect her leadership by emphasizing her role in the church.[13]

He concluded by saying that many were impacted by her servant leadership; Phoebe was a highly respected, entrusted influencer!

I can't imagine Paul telling Phoebe not to lead or to be quiet in church!

Was she flawless? I imagine not. Just an ordinary woman, like you and me. A woman who embraced the entrusted call of God on her life.

Say her name out loud: Phoebe.

We stand on *her* shoulders.

## Priscilla and Her Husband, Aquila

*Greet Priscilla and Aquila, my co-workers in Christ*
*Jesus. They risked their lives for me. Not only I but*
*all the churches of the Gentiles are grateful to them.*
*Greet also the church that meets at their house.*

—Romans 16:3–5

Did you know that Priscilla and Aquila's partnership is highlighted six times—one of the first husband-and-wife ministry teams! I completely resonate with their story, as my husband and I have shared more than four decades of ministry side by side.

Interestingly, Priscilla is mentioned first in four of the six instances, deviating from the Roman custom of the male being mentioned first, potentially indicating Priscilla's prominence in the ministry partnership.[14]

Early church father John Chrysostom (347–407) acknowledged that Priscilla was singled out when he wrote:

> This too is worthy of inquiry, why, as he addressed
> them, Paul has placed Priscilla before her husband.
> For he did not say, "Greet Aquila and Priscilla," but
> "Priscilla and Aquila." He does not do this without a
> reason, but he seems to me to acknowledge a greater
> godliness for her than for her husband.[15]

Priscilla's name is also mentioned before Aquila's in the account of how they instructed the brilliant orator and teacher Apollos in Ephesus (Acts 18:26), which has led many scholars to believe Priscilla played an instrumental role in instructing him.[16]

Priscilla and Aquila were both counted among Paul's closest ministry partners and devoted disciples. They are depicted in Acts 18 not only as being fellow tentmakers but as playing crucial roles alongside Paul in his missionary journeys when he established churches in Corinth and Ephesus (1 Cor. 16:19). Paul continued traveling, but the couple remained in Ephesus to nurture the new church (Acts 18:19).

Although he didn't give all the details in Romans 16, Paul acknowledged that Priscilla and Aquila risked their lives for him, earning gratitude not only from Paul but also from *all the Gentile churches*!

I'm sure Priscilla and Aquila faced challenges similar to any husband-wife team today. While acknowledging Priscilla's role as a woman, I am in no way disregarding the influence of Aquila, a man confident enough in his own gifts to celebrate hers.

Together their combined strengths shook hell and built the early church.

They led together. On the #sameteam. *Both* were church planters and significant leaders in the early church.

With that in mind, I can't imagine Paul telling Priscilla to be quiet and not lead. Can you?

Together, they pushed through obstacles we may never know about this side of heaven and persisted in building the church as a husband-and-wife team.

Say their names out loud: Priscilla and Aquila!

We stand on *their* shoulders.

## Junia and Andronicus

*Greet Andronicus and Junia, my fellow Jews who have been in prison with me. They are outstanding among the apostles, and they were in Christ before I was.*

—Romans 16:7

For years, I overlooked Junia's name, but she undoubtedly deserves deeper reflection. According to Paul's writings, Junia and Andronicus (her husband or brother) were followers of Jesus before Paul's conversion. Whether they were eyewitnesses of Jesus or converts after his resurrection, their friendship, influence, and partnership with Paul were significant.

Many of us don't know about Junia because in the thirteenth century, a patriarchal interpretation suggested Junia was a male. This error continued until recent scholarship uncovered that she was indeed a woman![17]

Not only was Junia a cellmate of Paul's (they were in prison for preaching the gospel), but Paul called Junia and Andronicus *apostles*, a designation he used for himself. Describing them as "outstanding among the apostles" (Rom. 16:7), Paul's comment leads us to see that he did not look at her gender as prohibitive but considered only her and Andronicus's devotion, giftedness, and calling.

Even John Chrysostom, who lived during the fourth and fifth centuries, recognized recognized the enormity of Paul's praise. He wrote:

> To be an apostle is something great. But to be outstanding among the apostles—just think what a wonderful song of praise that is! They [Junia and

Andronicus] were outstanding on the basis of their works and virtuous actions. Indeed, how great the wisdom of this woman must have been that she was even deemed worthy of the title of apostle.[18]

This mention of Junia as a female apostle in Romans 16:7 holds immense weight as it dismantles the argument that Paul excluded women from church leadership and teaching.

Let's consider this for a moment: Paul emphasized the pivotal role of apostles as "the foundation" of the church (Eph. 2:20) as they were the ones responsible for establishing churches and instructing early converts.

Scot McKnight, a New Testament scholar, writes this about Junia: "She was in essence a Christ-experiencing, Christ-representing, church-establishing, probably miracle-working, missionizing woman who preached the gospel and taught the church."[19]

Junia and Andronicus were a female-male ministry team who figured out how to use their gifts together to build the church. Empowered by the Holy Spirit and mutually submitted to one another (v. 5:21), they functioned in oneness to steward what had been entrusted to them.

Their story should encourage all of us, igniting within us a relentless passion, to make an impact advancing the kingdom of God regardless of the personal sacrifices it entails. Junia and Andronicus's commitment to steward their entrustment is an inspiration for how both genders can serve together.

Sounds a bit like Eden before the fall and a picture of the new creation, right?

I can't imagine Paul telling Junia to keep silent and not lead. Can you?

Say her name out loud with me: Junia!

We stand on her shoulders.

## Lydia

> *On the Sabbath we went outside the city gate to the river, where we expected to find a place of prayer. We sat down and began to speak to the women who had gathered there. One of those listening was a woman from the city of Thyatira named Lydia, a dealer in purple cloth. She was a worshiper of God. The Lord opened her heart to respond to Paul's message. When she and the members of her household were baptized, she invited us to her home. "If you consider me a believer in the Lord," she said, "come and stay at my house." And she persuaded us.*
>
> —Acts 16:13–15

I'm excited for you to discover more about Lydia's story as an influential businesswoman. During Paul and Silas's initial missionary journey, they visited Philippi, a prominent Roman province in Macedonia. During the Sabbath prayer meeting outside the city gates by the river, Paul engaged in conversation with a group of praying women. Lydia, captivated by Paul's gospel message, opened her heart to God, which led to her being baptized along with her entire household. This moment marked the beginning of Christianity in Philippi, with Lydia as its first convert.

Lydia is not only described as a worshipper of God but also a seller of purple cloth, which meant she was a businesswoman dealing in luxury textiles. The exclusive use of Tyrian purple dye, sourced from rare marine mollusks, was a symbol of affluence reserved for the wealthy elite who adorned their clothing and home furnishings with it. Although we don't know whether she inherited a family business or started her own, we do know Lydia was a wealthy and influential woman.

Lydia's wealth and influence are also indicated by the presumed ownership of her own home, where she hosted Paul and Silas (v. 15). During their stay, she likely became a disciple of Paul and Silas, receiving theological teaching and guidance from these two church planters.

Additionally, Luke tells us that Paul and Silas "went to Lydia's house, where they met with the brothers and sisters and encouraged them" (Acts 16:40), indicating that the first house church[20] in Philippi met in Lydia's home, and she was the leader.[21]

This took courage, creativity, and inspiration. She was gifted with a calling of entrepreneurship and used those gifts to build the church.

This tells me there is room for you, friend.

If you are a businesswoman leading a thriving corporation or a hopeful entrepreneur launching a fledgling start-up, your unique God-given gifts are vital for the kingdom.

You have no idea the impact and echo of what your courageous yes can mean for generations that will be influenced by you.

God has uniquely shaped you for what he's entrusted to you; your history, failures, successes, and pain are all part of your story.

Lydia's yes echoes over you as *you* pioneer and stay faithful to the call.

Also, let's not miss that she was the *first* recorded convert in Europe.

Consider for a moment the magnificent cathedrals scattered across Europe and the rich history of the church. If we were to trace their origins back to the first convert, it would perhaps lead us to one woman's profound surrender to Christ: Lydia.

Undoubtedly, Lydia faced incredible challenges answering his call on her life, and you will too. Despite the obstacles Lydia faced, her resolute surrender, her unequivocal yes, still echoes loudly today.

Say her name out loud: Lydia.

We stand on her shoulders.

## Tryphena, Tryphosa, Persis, and Mary

*Greet Tryphena and Tryphosa, those women who work hard in the Lord. Greet my dear friend Persis, another woman who has worked very hard in the Lord.*

—Romans 16:12

*Greet Mary, who worked very hard for you.*

—Romans 16:6

Although the details about these women are sparse, Paul commended them for their hard work in contributing to the establishment of the church in Rome. Even though we don't have specifics, the mere mention of their names is extraordinary.

New Testament scholar Dr. Kevin Giles suggests that "the word translated 'worked hard' is the Greek verb *kopiaō*.... Paul frequently uses the verb *kopiaō* when speaking of the ministry of those involved in teaching and preaching."[22]

Whether these women were teachers and preachers or served in other various capacities, Paul considered them ministry partners deserving of respect. They didn't sit back on the sidelines or take it easy but used what they'd been entrusted with to see God's love infiltrate their communities. In a culture that often overlooked the roles and actions of women, these four were remarkable contributors who stood out. Paul was determined to make sure that the church in Rome recognized and honored them for their valuable contributions.

They pushed past the obstacles and gave their all.

I can't imagine Paul telling them to be quiet ...

Go ahead and say their names out loud: Tryphena, Tryphosa, Persis, Mary.

We stand on their shoulders.

## Lois and Eunice

> *I am reminded of your sincere faith, which first lived*
> *in your grandmother Lois and in your mother Eunice*
> *and, I am persuaded, now lives in you also.*
> *For this reason I remind you to fan into flame the gift of*
> *God, which is in you through the laying on of my hands.*
> —2 Timothy 1:5–6

Timothy was Paul's protégé and spiritual son who traveled with him, eventually becoming the pastor of the church in Ephesus. In Paul's second letter to Timothy, the church was grappling with division, false doctrine, and persecution.

What stands out in this mention of Timothy's mother and grandmother is the incredible impact of their teaching *on him*—their sincere and unwavering faith capable of enduring trials. Timothy's mother was a Jewish believer, and his father was Greek (Acts 16:1–3; 1 Tim. 1:3).

This suggests that Timothy was spiritually nurtured by his mother and grandmother shaping him into an outstanding leader. Their spiritual influence was evidenced in Timothy's leadership potential as a young man; Paul considered Timothy capable of accompanying him and eventually leading the church in Ephesus.

This is for all the mamas and grandmothers reading this. You don't need a platform or a spotlight; your potential and impact in building the church and impacting the world lies in the words you speak to your sons and daughters and grandchildren and through the prayers you pray. Keep instilling in them a sincere and unwavering faith, empowering them to stand strong in whatever God calls them to, and don't underestimate your influence. There's great power in a praying mama or grandmother!

Paul's message to Timothy was clear: Don't forget the sincere faith from your mother and grandmother, and fan into flame those gifts you received through the laying on of my hands.

The leaders in the next generation need a Lois, a Eunice, *and* a Paul speaking over them and reminding them to fan the flame of what God has entrusted to them. Spiritual mothers *and* fathers are both needed to build the church.

Speak their names out loud: Lois and Eunice.

We stand on their shoulders today.

## The Four Unnamed Prophesying Daughters of Philip the Evangelist

*Leaving the next day, we reached Caesarea and stayed at the house of Philip the evangelist, one of the Seven. He had four unmarried daughters who prophesied.*

—Acts 21:8–9

> *In the last days, God says,*
> *I will pour out my Spirit on all people.*
> *Your sons* and daughters *will prophesy,*
> *your young men will see visions,*
> *your old men will dream dreams.*
> *Even on my servants, both men and women,*
> *I will pour out my Spirit in those days,*
> *and* they will prophesy.
>
> —Acts 2:17–18

Luke's intentional mention of these four unmarried women prophesying, which is a vocal gift, is worth looking at more closely. First, Luke underscored and celebrated that the women had a voice. Second, this is for all you who have ever felt disqualified from ministry because you aren't married. It's not your marital status that qualifies you; it's your yes to whatever God is asking you to do.

I also don't want to miss the significance that, among all the Old Testament references to what was happening on the day of Pentecost, Peter chose the book of Joel, which mentions the Spirit giving voice to *both* genders. Keep in mind, this was Peter's first sermon on the day the New Testament church was birthed, laying a foundation for us all.

Theologian Amos Yong writes, "Furthermore, from the perspective of the day of Pentecost, the role of women in Luke-Acts is a fulfillment of Joel's prophecy regarding the Spirit being given fully also to women (cf. Joel 2:28–29; Acts 2:17)."[23] Luke and Paul apparently took the presence of female Christian prophets for granted, mentioning them without the need for any defense or commentary (Luke 2:36–38; Acts 21:8–9; 1 Cor. 11:5; 14:29–32).

The Bible clearly portrays women functioning under the authority of the Holy Spirit, with the gifts of the Holy Spirit, standing as equal recipients, alongside men, of the promise of the Spirit. This reaffirms that God empowers women, gives us a voice, and entrusts us with gifts by his Spirit.

Even without their specific names to say out loud ...

We stand on these prophesying daughters' shoulders!

## Pioneers

The women we've looked at in this chapter, and many others,[24] partnered with Paul or played pivotal roles in the birth of the early church. Alongside their male counterparts, they were bold, passionate, wise, and courageous under persecution, standing on the frontlines using the gifts entrusted to them by Christ.

Now that we've navigated some of the *descriptive* verses outlining who they were, we must wrestle with the corrective and instructive verses that have been used to silence women.

Okay. Here we go.

Time to wrestle with the text.

I can't wait for you to see these verses through a new lens.

But before we do ...

These women whom Paul wrote about in his letters were *ezer* women, just like the ones I mentioned from the Old Testament. They are examples for us to follow, shoulders we can stand on. Let's not be the generation that forgets what's been given to us by becoming overfamiliar with the calling and the cost others have paid throughout history for what we've been entrusted with.

In fact, consider some of the *ezer* women who were pioneers in just the first five hundred years of the church and the cost they paid:

- Thecla, an early second century female evangelist martyred for her faith.[25]
- Monica, the mother of the influential philosopher and theologian Augustine of Hippo (354–430), was remembered by her son "for her tireless commitment to prayer for his salvation, her bright mind for philosophical dialogue, and her maturity in faith that drew them both into communion with God."[26]
- Perpetua and Felicity, whose testimony "I am a Christian" led to their martyrdom as they faced beasts in an arena. St. Augustine called them "God's holy servants."[27]
- Blandina, a slave who was also martyred. She lived in Lugdunum (southern France) and was tortured and killed for her faith in the Amphitheater of the Three Gauls.[28]
- Macrina, "who guided her brothers, [influential theologians] Gregory of Nyssa and Basil of Caesarea, in spiritual and philosophical teachings."[29] This fourth-century dynamo was also an emancipator of slaves.[30]

These women gave their lives for the sake of the gospel. While I don't have room in this book to mention all of them, there are thousands whose names you may never know.

I am grateful for the pioneers who have gone before us, so many who have given me courage and inspiration.

> Let's not be the generation that forgets what's been given to us by becoming overfamiliar with the calling and the cost others have paid throughout history for what we've been entrusted with.

Let's not be the generation that forgets we stand on *their* shoulders.

Did they all do this perfectly?

Absolutely not.

Neither have I.

And neither will you.

But if perfection is your goal, you'll never get started. An imperfect yes is much better than an excuse not to start.

Pioneering is not for the faint of heart. God has called you to this moment in history. (Thankfully we have indoor plumbing and don't have to wear lace petticoats!) Yet you must decide if you're up for this.

So, two important questions as we end this chapter.

Whose shoulders do you stand on? We may never know her as you do, but go ahead and say *her name* out loud right now ...

Who will stand on your shoulders as you continue to pioneer what God has entrusted to you?

## Hineni

*Here I am, Lord. Use me. I am so challenged and grateful for the women who have pioneered and lived a life of great personal sacrifice to build the kingdom of God.*

Take this moment to personalize your hineni prayer of surrender. What areas do you need to surrender so you can be the leader God has called you to be?

...................................................................................................

...................................................................................................

...................................................................................................

...................................................................................................

...................................................................................................

...................................................................................................

...................................................................................................

*I say yes to all you have for me. Hineni.*

## Chapter 7

# Don't Be a Karen

*It is time for us to rethink some of our oldest beliefs and traditions. It is time for us to repent for whatever ways we have hindered God's work and misread His Word. It is time for us to release women to be all that God has called them to be.*

—Loren Cunningham

Don't be a Karen.

Unless, of course, your real name is Karen. Then obviously, please be a Karen. There is only one you; don't trade that for someone else.

In recent years, the term *Karen* has become derogatory slang used to describe an irritable middle-aged woman who is perceived as exhibiting entitled or demanding behavior that goes beyond what is considered appropriate. The term is frequently depicted in memes that portray these women leveraging their privilege to assert their own desires. These memes often involve someone who is insisting on speaking to the manager, sporting a specific bob hairstyle, or displaying racist behavior. We know that every form of racism is heartbreaking and wrong, so I don't want to dilute the fact that many of the memes of a Karen depict this behavior.

But I also don't want to miss that we can all carry the posture of a Karen if we're not careful, regardless of our race, economic or social status, or gender.

We can all feel entitled rather than entrusted.

What if the message at the heart of Paul's challenging instructions to women (and the church) is that they should not have an entitled posture but remember what they've been entrusted with?

Not a posture of privilege but humility.

I don't know about you, but I don't want to be remembered as a Karen.

I hope you've started awakening to your value as a woman and are hearing the echo from heaven over you. Whether your assignment right now is CEO, entrepreneur, lawyer, stay-at-home mom, educator, pastor, student, leader in your church or community—no matter your role in your current season—I hope you're learning these two things:

> You are seen, loved, and valued by God; nothing about you is insignificant to him.

> We've been entrusted together on the #sameteam—men and women—and we stand on the shoulders of those who've pioneered before us.

Here we are at the final chapter in section 1. Well done—you've made it this far!

Now we've landed at the most contested verses about women.

Are you curious?

All the biggest conflicts have a backstory. Whether it's the latest celebrity feud captivating social media or the story behind World War II, the details are essential to understanding what all the fuss is about.

Because who doesn't love the juicy details behind a conflict?

I know I do. We're going to go behind the scenes and "spill the tea" so you have a deeper understanding.

Let's set the stage first.

## A Breathtaking Theology

As we dive into Paul's letters to the house churches he established, it's essential to acknowledge him as a spiritual father providing guidance and support amid their unique challenges. Whether the new converts came from synagogues or pagan worship, they were pioneering completely new concepts of fellowship that differed vastly from what they were accustomed to, and with that came a boatload of issues.

A full boatload.

Whether you're currently a leader or influencer or aspiring to be one, you've likely wrestled with a similar boatload, straining to keep the ship afloat and moving toward its destination. Paul's timeless messages resonate because the issues he addressed are similar to those that churches and organizations face today; humanity, at its core, is imperfect and needs a Savior.

But hear me: If you don't know the original issue Paul was referring to, you might be confused about whether the verses were absolute truth for all time for all people or instruction for a specific situation in the church he was writing to.

While much of the Western world increasingly considers men and women equal in terms of value or essence, the conflict remains focused on where they share equal roles. We'll discover that, in fact, Paul wrote only a few verses that have been used for centuries to silence women and limit their roles, compared to the beautiful story in his letters that describes both genders serving together as co-stewards of the gifts entrusted to them.

How Paul modeled this theology is breathtaking by the sheer number of women that he led with given the cultural context in which he lived.

This chapter will go a little deeper into details we might miss if we don't dig into the biblical language and context.

Whether you've been curious and eagerly waiting for this type of study or you feel like I did (just two brain cells short of smart), I am confident God is going to speak to you within these pages!

## When a Muffin *Isn't* a Muffin

We'll get down to business in a second, but first let me share an incredibly humiliating story that drives home the importance of accurately interpreting language and context.

A number of years ago, our church partnered with several churches in our area to host an annual women's conference called The Rising at Constitution Hall in the heart of DC. It was an incredible experience to see so many women touched by the powerful worship that resounded throughout this historic building, along with inspiring messages from gifted speakers and the tangible presence of God.

We had just finished a deeply moving moment with an announcement that our conference had raised a significant amount of money to donate to A21,[1] an organization dedicated to fighting human trafficking. My role was to transition this moment into a lighter one as the women were being released for a break. As I walked onto the platform, I asked everyone to stand and then brilliantly said:

"Now I want you to lean over to the girl next to you and pinch your girlfriend's muffin."

What in the world?!

I meant to say, "Pinch your girlfriend's cheeks," but I got a bit flustered and nervous in the moment, and my brain switched that sentence to "Pinch your girlfriend's muffin top," which is crazy enough. But what I heard my mouth say was "Pinch your girlfriend's muffin."

Everyone started laughing, and because I didn't really know what I was saying, I repeated it amid the roaring laughter that engulfed the room. *Then* I told them they could go home after this and tell their husbands and friends, "I pinched my girlfriend's muffin."

More hysterical laughter.

Here's the significant thing I didn't know that this room of urban millennials already knew. *Muffin* now means more than the blueberry or banana baked good you have for breakfast. In modern slang, *muffin* means "vagina."

So, yes. Apparently, I had just told this room full of women to pinch their girlfriend's vagina.

*Now* it's hilarious ... but in the moment, I was mortified.

I still cringe at the words that spilled from my mouth when it seemed to be disconnected from my brain!

So, just a wee reminder before we keep going. Oftentimes, we don't pick ourselves for what God is asking us to do because of what's on repeat in our minds: the moments we failed to do things perfectly.

As you keep reading, friends, I hope you are letting go of whatever "muffin story" you might carry. And I hope you're able to read this knowing God wants to ignite a *yes* in you for whatever he is asking you to do, not despite your imperfections but because of them. The story of how God redeems your greatest failures and removes the soundtrack of shame is what we all need to hear.

And it is how God's story is woven into yours.

Needless to say, how words are translated and defined is essential, and what we sometimes take at face value often has a different meaning.

Here we go. Ready for the "tea" behind the conflict?

I want to make sure you don't miss any inaccurately translated "muffins" hidden in the text.

Go ahead and pick your pen up and take notes on what God speaks to you as you read. I am going to activate your brain and your heart.

I want this chapter to mark you.

## Houston, We Have a Problem!

*I also want the women to dress modestly, with*
*decency and propriety, adorning themselves,*
*not with elaborate hairstyles or gold or pearls or*
*expensive clothes, but with good deeds, appropriate*
*for women who profess to worship God.*
*A woman should learn in quietness and full submission.*
*I do not permit a woman to teach or to assume authority*
*over a man; she must be quiet. For Adam was formed*
*first, then Eve. And Adam was not the one deceived; it*
*was the woman who was deceived and became a sinner.*

*But women will be saved through childbearing—if they*
*continue in faith, love and holiness with propriety.*
—1 Timothy 2:9–15

Sheesh, those are some strong words to swallow!

You'll most likely recognize these verses, as many debates on gender roles hinge on a literal interpretation of 1 Timothy 2:11–12. Yet, if we only focus on a few verses from Paul's writings, claiming they are *absolute truth for all women forever* without *considering the specific context* in which he wrote them, then a potential problem arises.

We've already seen that the New Testament describes women as active participants in ministry. Now we see a few verses that advocate for the complete silence of women.

Houston, we have a problem!

So. Much. Tension.

Are you confused? As you know by now, I am not going to ignore the tension but am going to invite you to sit in it as we dig.

The first highly contested verses we'll look at are from Paul's letter to Timothy when Timothy was leading the new church plant in Ephesus:

"A woman should learn in quietness and full submission. I do not permit a woman to teach or to assume authority over a man; she must be quiet" (1 Tim. 2:11–12).

The theologian N. T. Wright contends that we can't ignore the specific context for the recipients of Paul's letter in Ephesus. Wright believes there was a possibility this letter was instructive for women coming out of the cult of Diana (Artemis),[2] which taught that women

were superior to men.[3] These women needed discipleship on how
to serve *alongside* men with humility rather than the domineering
characteristic of the cult.[4] Lucy Peppiatt, principal of Westminster
Theological Centre, agrees that a careful study of the religious environ-
ment of Ephesus in the first century is important: "The idea that Paul
was addressing an early heresy in the Ephesian church propagated by a
few influential women converts from the Artemis cult also helps us to
make sense of what was written."[5] Sandra Glahn, a professor at Dallas
Theological Seminary, adds that Paul "has the teachings of the Artemis
cult in mind when he writes to his protégé."[6] Recent research studying
the ancient culture of Artemis alongside literary works of the time[7]
provides even more insight into what Timothy may have been facing.[8]

The conflict surrounding these verses arises when scholars isolate
them from the rest of the chapter as the only ones to be taken literally. If we take a literal approach for the entire passage, then the dress
code (vv. 9–10) would be advising women against wearing jewelry or
expensive clothing. In essence Walmart, Goodwill, Amazon, or Target
would be the best bet to find your outfit of the day, while Neiman Mar-
cus, Gucci, and that wedding ring would be off-limits!

While I always love a good Target find, I don't interpret this as a
*literal* dress code, and most likely neither do you!

Here's the scoop behind Paul's detailed encouragement on what
to wear. Some scholars believed Ephesus had a reputation for pro-
miscuity, suggesting a link between immodest dress and behavior.[9]
Yet recent research indicates that Paul was likely instructing women
not to emulate the sensual, or wealth- and status-displaying, attire of
Artemis worshippers, including braided hairstyles.[10] In this context,
Paul urged women to avoid dressing provocatively or in a manner that

flaunted their social status. He emphasized that, as followers of Christ, we should wear attire that reflects *inner* values demonstrated through "good deeds" (v. 10).

Hear me: Paul was not saying you must dress like a pioneer woman and not be fashionable! But rather, "regardless of what else you put on, wear love. It's your basic, all-purpose garment. Never be without it" (Col. 3:12–14 MSG).

Perhaps you're thinking the same thing as me: picking only one verse out of a passage for literal interpretation is faulty hermeneutics (a fancy word for the study or principles of interpretation of the text).

Another tension exists in Paul's encouragement to "learn in quietness" (1 Tim. 2:11). This seems to contradict 1 Corinthians 11:2–6 (more details later in this chapter), where Paul instructed women about praying and prophesying in corporate worship.[11]

Let's not overlook that Paul's statement in 1 Timothy 2:11 echoes Jesus' acceptance of women's learning: "A woman should *learn* in quietness and full submission." The word for "learn" (*manthanetō*) is the root for "disciple." As we saw in chapter 4, women—not commonly disciples of a rabbi—had limited access to teaching, rendering them susceptible to believing and repeating false teachings. Perhaps Paul was referring to women coming from pagan worship, who were combining what they believed from Artemis worship with the truth Paul was teaching.[12] Paul's desire for women to learn, be discipled, and filled with knowledge of the truth (1 Tim. 2:4) aimed not only at preventing the spread of false teachings (influenced by the Artemis cult) but also to educate women in culturally appropriate ways.

Paul (and Jesus) consistently confronted cultural norms to empower women; these weren't one-time exceptions but patterns to follow.

Also, noteworthy: If Paul truly endorsed the complete silence of women, why didn't he rebuke Priscilla instead of commending her for teaching Apollos "the way of God more adequately" in Ephesus (Acts 18:26)? According to Paul, her joint leadership with Aquila was vital for the church plant.

It doesn't make sense, does it?

But let's keep digging deeper. There is so much gold in this passage!

Paul switched from referring to men and women (plural) in 1 Timothy 2:8–10 to speaking about man and woman (singular)[13] in verses 11 and 12 (learn quietly and don't teach or assume authority), which may suggest he was writing to Timothy regarding a specific couple.[14] If this is the case, the verses contain instructions for a particular couple and not all women *forever*. We must consider this probability because otherwise, based on what we've already seen in Paul's ministry, it would directly contradict what Paul wrote later to Timothy: "And the things you have heard me say in the presence of many witnesses *entrust* to reliable *people*[15] who will also be qualified to teach others" (2 Tim. 2:2).

So then, what do we do with the Adam and Eve verses and the "women will be saved through childbearing" part (1 Tim. 2:13–15)? I've always been confused by this particular passage because I was never saved in any way birthing my four children, except perhaps in living through it!

Considering the context, some scholars suggest that, in addressing the Genesis story, Paul was combating two specific false teachings from the Artemis cult. He was correcting the belief that women were the originators of man by reaffirming the creation story order.

Additionally, Paul was dispelling the false teaching that Artemis was the savior of women in labor by emphasizing God's protection for those who trust in him during childbearing.[16]

Doesn't this make so much more sense? Whether Paul was instructing a specific couple or imparting instruction to the entire church, his intent was that they understood the truth concerning God.

A third tension for consideration from 1 Timothy 2:12 is the Greek word *hesuchia*. Gail Wallace maintains, "It has been translated as 'silent' for centuries in many English translations of the Bible, but a more accurate translation would be 'quietly' or 'in quietness.' Paul used this term in 2 Thessalonians 3:12, instructing the church to 'settle down.'"[17] The translation leans more to a posture of being calm, tranquil or settled.[18] This thought is consistent in his first letter to Timothy, where he wrote to "live peaceful and quiet lives" (v. 2:2).

In this light, Paul doesn't seem to be advocating for complete silence but is encouraging a gentle and peaceful disposition with a receptive attitude.[19] Paul was guiding women *how* to engage in the learning process in a public setting of a house church!

Perhaps the most challenging issue in this passage stems from the Greek word *authentein*, translated in most Bibles as "authority" (v. 12).

*Authentein* is a unique Greek verb used only once in Scripture and when used in extrabiblical texts was often associated with aggression. Greek dictionaries offer the translation "to control in a domineering manner,"[20] or "to have control over or to domineer."[21] Because it is used only once in the Bible, it is necessary to consult the other literature and the cultural context in that era for meaning.

Examining this term in the context of Ephesus, women influenced by the Artemis cult believed in their superiority over men. Possibly, as they followed Jesus, they still had a self-centered, domineering posture.

Many scholars believe a better translation of what Paul was saying to women was not a prohibition on leadership generally, but rather an admonition not to teach in a domineering way.

In other words, don't be a Karen when speaking or leading.

Just want to make sure you didn't miss this. Because the cultural Karen we see in memes—that irritated middle-aged woman who feels entitled to more—who wants *her* on their team?

I don't, and you probably don't either.

Paul was saying if you're going to lead, whether female or male, your leadership posture should be one of humility and entrustment.

We've all seen enough women—and men for that matter—in leadership who act entitled, whether it's because they felt they haven't been heard, have experienced past pain, or lack self-awareness.

That's the exact opposite posture of how God is asking us to live as entrusted influencers!

Last but not least, it's crucial to understand this word *authentein* (1 Tim. 2:12) is a *hapax legomenon*, which refers to a word that occurs only once in an author's writings. This makes it challenging, if not impossible, to precisely infer the writer's intended meaning because there are no other examples of that word usage for comparison. So, when translating the meaning of *authentein* as "authority," we must be cautious about using this verse as a basis for doctrine.[22]

Go ahead and let the phrase *hapax legomenon* roll around in your mouth for a minute. Then practice saying it out loud.

Just think how smart you'll sound the next time you're at lunch, when you mention how *authentein* is a *hapax legomenon* and how your life goal is to be an entrusted influencer in company with generations of *ezer* women.

And not a Karen.

## So ... Do We Have Permission or Not?

> *Let your women keep silence in the churches: for*
> *it is not permitted unto them to speak; but they*
> *are commanded to be under obedience as also*
> *saith the law. And if they will learn any thing,*
> *let them ask their husbands at home: for it is*
> *a shame for women to speak in the church.*
> —1 Corinthians 14:34–35 KJV

What is it? Do we stay silent or do we follow the examples Paul described in the early church?

Sounds so confusing *again*, right?

Let's stay curious and take this as an invitation to lean into the tension of what Paul was implying. God isn't disturbed by your questions; in fact, he invites them. Remember, Jesus asked more than three hundred recorded questions in the three years of his ministry![23]

So then, was Paul double-minded in how he led?

If we look at how Paul's teaching on the gifts of the Spirit in 1 Corinthians 12–14 is inclusive of both genders, it is difficult to comprehend why he would tell women to keep silent and not speak because some of those gifts are *vocal* gifts.

Paul's letter was from a spiritual father to the house churches in Corinth in response to some issues. Let's not miss that he was instructing them on the gifts of the Spirit—an entirely new concept for the church! He was teaching them not only how to use the gifts but also how to bring order in a church service (14:33).

From what we already discovered, since Paul gave instruction to women who were prophesying and praying (11:5), we must trust that his intent wasn't to permanently silence women. Instead, he was prohibiting *disruptive* speech.[24]

Additionally, if we take these verses literally, then women shouldn't be speaking in church at all, whether in the church lobby, the auditorium, or the spaces where the community interacts and connects.

And that doesn't make sense, does it?

So, what do we do with the conflict and tension that arises from these few verses?

We're going to take another holistic approach as we look at how Paul described women before we look at this passage that seems to be instructing and correcting them.

Before we address the instructions for women to keep silent in church, let's look in the same letter at the verses where Paul encouraged women to speak to see what was being echoed over the women in Corinth.

Philip Payne, author of *The Bible vs. Biblical Womanhood*, maintains that before we get to the difficult-to-understand verses in this epistle, we must remember that Paul "repeatedly asserts that God gives spiritual gifts to all believers" in 1 Corinthians 12:7–11.[25] There is no distinction between men and women; the Spirit decides to whom the gifts are distributed. While he wrote about apostles, prophets, and teachers, nowhere in this chapter did Paul put gender restrictions on gifts. In fact, 1 Corinthians 12 opens with Paul inviting both genders into his teaching on the gifts of the Spirit: "Now about the gifts of the Spirit, *brothers and sisters*, I do not want you to be uninformed" (v. 1).

To emphasize this further, consider Paul's inclusive language of encouragement throughout this letter to the church in Corinth:

> "I would like *every one of you* to ... prophesy." (14:5)

> "But if an unbeliever or an inquirer comes in while *everyone is prophesying*, they are convicted of sin and are brought under judgment by all." (14:24)

> "What then shall we say, *brothers and sisters*? When you come together, *each of you* has a hymn, or a word of instruction, a revelation, a tongue or an interpretation." (14:26)

> "For *you can all prophesy* in turn so that everyone may be instructed and encouraged." (14:31)

> "But *every woman* who prays or prophesies ..." (11:5)

> "Therefore, my *brothers and sisters, be eager to prophesy*." (14:39)

While some scholars have maintained this prophetic vocal gift for women didn't take place in the public setting of a church, in

1 Corinthians 14:4 Paul wrote, "The one who prophesies edifies the *church*."

Taking one verse to silence all women for all time is, again, faulty hermeneutics, when we also observe Paul's non-gender-specific encouragement in Colossians 3:16 (KJV) to "let the word of Christ dwell in you richly in all wisdom; *teaching and admonishing* one another in psalms and hymns and spiritual songs."

This sounds to me like the "Go tell" for women from the lips of Jesus and the first sermon on the day of Pentecost, where both genders were encouraged to use their vocal gifts, were echoing over this early church!

A second tension in this passage is that the Greek word for "silence," *sigao,* is different from the word Paul used in 1 Timothy 2:11–12. While similar in meaning, *silence* here signifies having a listening posture and not creating a disturbance while learning, not complete silence in church![26]

Remember, Christianity was brand-new in Corinth and this entire revelation from Paul that taught everyone to use their spiritual gifts was revolutionary. Since Christian women were given a voice, not devalued or marginalized as they were in the rest of the culture, they were flocking to these newly formed house churches[27] and, for the first time, in need of instruction in these public gatherings.

Now that we've established women could be disciples and that Paul was referring to a posture of listening, what do we do with the tension of the "learn at home" part (1 Cor. 14:35)?

This is still a bit troublesome.

In Greek and Jewish settings, interruptions during teaching were common, often involving questions from the listeners. Due to the general lack of education among women, Paul suggested they wait to ask questions at home to avoid disrupting the meeting as they were new to this concept.

> *Silence* here signifies having a listening posture and not creating a disturbance while learning, not complete silence in church!

Dr. Craig Keener maintains, "When Paul suggests that husbands should teach their wives at home, his point is not to belittle women's ability to learn. To the contrary, Paul is advocating the most progressive view of his day: despite the possibility that she is less educated than himself, the husband should recognize his wife's intellectual capability and therefore make himself responsible for her education, so they can discuss intellectual issues together."[28]

Decades ago, when I devoted my life to Christ, my husband, already a seasoned Christian, became my mentor. Our ongoing conversations have been a beautiful dialogue of discovery and mutually shared insights.

This is what Paul was advising the church—invest in collaborative learning to grow together. And if you're single or lack such dialogue with a spouse, find someone in your local church to discuss the Word of God with beyond your Sunday experience. It will enhance your depth of understanding as it did for those in the early church.

As we look at this verse with fresh eyes, simple deduction tells us that perhaps Paul was dealing with a specific issue in Corinth as he was when he was writing to Timothy in Ephesus.

Are you wondering, like me, how we have been so oblivious to the obvious?

Keener also makes this wise proposal: "It would be surprising if an issue that would exclude at least half of the body of Christ from a ministry of teaching would be addressed in only one text, unless that text really addressed only a specific historical situation rather than setting forth a universal prohibition."

Keener concludes, "Paul wants them [women] to learn so that they could *teach*. If he prohibits women from teaching because they are unlearned, his demand that they learn constitutes a long-range solution."[29]

The realization that Paul was advocating for a long-term solution rather than silencing women is truly remarkable.

So then, is it possible there is no limitation because of gender in any of what Paul wrote to the Corinthian church?

We've only scratched the surface of two highly contested passages, but I wanted to give you a glimpse into how Paul empowered women and was echoing God's heart for you.

Mind-blowing, hey?

Have we perhaps misinterpreted the "muffins" along the way, perceiving a discouraging tone in Paul's voice concerning women, when in fact he and God are our greatest advocates?

Paul was literally flipping the culture on its flipping head because *he saw the significance of women leading alongside men*!

## As Dearly Loved Children

I love how Paul urged the Ephesians to "follow God's example, therefore, as dearly loved children" (Eph. 5:1).

Frankly, without the constant awareness of being deeply loved by our heavenly Father, our efforts to "get it right" will become a mechanical checklist of performing for God.

We can't possibly follow the example of Jesus, or Paul, if we don't remember that one thing. This intimate connection with God becomes our foundation to serve from and *the foundation for* God's entrustment of leadership to us.

Imagine with me, for a minute. What would it look like if our life motto was to "outdo one another in showing honor" (Rom. 12:10 ESV)?

What if *this* was the defining image for our leadership and influence?

Showing honor and submitting "*to one another* out of reverence for Christ" (Eph. 5:21) is the strongest muscle you can develop, especially as a leader or influencer. Romans 12:10 and Ephesians 5:21 are not gender-specific commands but directions to each of us to lead this way. But these muscles can develop only as we grow in the confidence that we are dearly loved children of the Father.

So perhaps your final takeaway from this chapter is to prioritize cultivating intimacy with God, and *then* the entrusted God-given gifts will naturally flow out of a posture that tries to "outdo one another in showing honor." Knowing we are dearly loved children silences the craving for recognition from others because we are already seen and loved by God.

What I know with certainty after all these years of ministry is that kind of *freedom* enables our influence in every arena to reach the next level!

## "I'm for Whatever God's Spirit Grants Women Gifts to Do"

Consider with me the implications that Jesus first entrusted a woman to "Go tell" about his resurrection. The Great Commission to make disciples, baptize, and teach (Matt. 28:19–20) isn't limited by gender, nor was the church when it was birthed on the day of Pentecost (Acts 2:17-18), and neither is using our gifts in any way gender restrictive.

What if we embraced women leading alongside men in our churches and work environments ... starting now?

That could usher in the emancipation of a generation of women who could lead alongside men and see the greatest harvest ever and the fulfillment of Psalm 68:11: "The Lord announces the word, and the women who proclaim it are a mighty throng."

Theologian Scot McKnight, author of *The Blue Parakeet,* tells this story of a conversation he had with F. F. Bruce, a respected New Testament scholar:

> "Professor Bruce, what do you think of women's ordination?"
>
> "I don't think the New Testament talks about ordination," he replied.
>
> "What about the silencing passages of Paul on women?" I asked.
>
> "I think Paul would roll over in his grave if he knew we were turning his letters into torah."
>
> *Wow!* I thought. *That's a good point to think about.* Thereupon I asked a question that he answered

in such a way that it reshaped my thinking: "What do you think, then, about women in church ministries?"

Professor Bruce's answer was as Pauline as Paul was: "I'm for whatever God's Spirit grants women gifts to do."[30]

## The Smart Ones

I told you I was going to spill the tea and reveal some of the behind-the-scenes, tension-filled details of this age-old conflict.

Well done making it to the end of section 1!

Did you learn anything?

For some of you, sitting in the tension has made you uncomfortable, maybe even irritated.

Good.

For others, you're sensing a permission-giving freedom from God for the first time.

Good.

Wherever you are on this journey of discovery, my desire in section 1 was to activate your brain and stir your heart with a curiosity to discover what the One who loves you most says about you, as a woman.

I can't wait for you to dive into section 2. You'll discover your own kind of smart and some practical tools for becoming the entrusted influencer God's called you to be. Things I wished I had known, but no one told me.

But before we move ahead …

What was your favorite discovery?

Learning what has been echoing over you from the first and second gardens? Discovering how the early church was built by both men and women?

How about all the *ezer* women whose shoulders we get to stand on?

I hope the margins of this book are filled with your notes. This should feel like a field manual for your future.

My prayer is that you feel smart.

*You*, my friend—the smart one because you're curious.

The one who will spend a lifetime learning.

The one who will never let your "certainty" in doctrine allow you to feel entitled but rather entrusted with truth.

The one constantly in awe that God would use imperfect girls like us.

The one who might not have picked yourself because you didn't feel qualified.

Yet God chose you and has uniquely entrusted you with gifts, strengths, and a story that he's going to use to silence shame and touch humanity.

Yes, you, friend.

You are here at this time in history for this moment. No matter how many tombstones are in your past or whether your present feels like a graveyard.

You are standing in the middle of your garden with your Rabboni, Jesus, the Head of the church, echoing over you and your sisters for thousands of generations. The ones who pioneered before you, the ones on whose shoulders you stand ...

Can you hear it from the One who loves you most?

"Go tell ..." There's resurrection in your mouth.

As I write this to you with a heart that is full, I sense the closeness of God in this sacred moment.

Here am I, Lord. Use me.

## Hineni

*No other response seems to be adequate for the magnitude of who you are and what you offer to me right now.*

*To me, Lord, the one who constantly lives feeling as if I am not enough.*

*Here I am, God.*

*I'm giving it all to you right now. I desire to be used by you, to live in the purpose you created me for. I surrender to you my limitations, weaknesses, strengths, and areas I don't understand. I give you the pain and the wounding I've experienced, and I ask you to forgive me for holding on to bitterness toward those who have hurt me, whether friends, family, mentors, or leaders.*

*I silence the soundtrack of shame and choose to stand in the confidence that I am loved and seen. I hear your echo and speak resurrection over the calling you've given me.*

*Here I am. Use me.*

# Section 2

# Introduction

## *What I Wish I'd Known That No One Told Me*

*If there ever comes a time when the women of the world
come together purely and simply for the benefit of mankind,
it will be a force such as the world has never known.*

—Matthew Arnold

I am a little dangerous with a tool chest.

But *not* because I am a woman.

However, my eldest daughter, Bethany, can wield a power tool with the best of them. In fact, on her twenty-first birthday, her favorite gift was the fully equipped toolbox her dad gave her. She was determined to fix everything with those tools. Bethany has become so good that if her dad's not around, she's the one I call to fix something. I am never sure which screwdriver or wrench to use, but she knows. I end up doing more harm than good with those tools because I never learned how to use them.

Knowing how to use the tools you've been given is essential.

Go ahead—dust yourself off and pat yourself on the back. Together we've just unearthed some profound biblical truths that are like owning a fully equipped toolbox.

You deserve a medal (or at the least an excavator license) for digging below the surface to begin clarifying the theology of what you believe and live. I hope it stirred you to think more deeply and made you hungry to put on a hard hat and start digging for yourself!

Did you learn anything in section 1 that confirmed God has entrusted you and wants to use your voice?

Good. I was hoping you would.

But now what do you do with that fully equipped toolbox?

Understanding *how* to use the information of entrusted leadership to build your life and better the lives of those around you is crucial. Otherwise, these tools can rust from sitting unused. Or if you don't know how to use and apply them, your influence will not reach its full potential and can do more harm than good.

There are so many things I wish I had known. Things I could have done better, quicker, and less painfully if someone had just been there to guide me.

Which is why this section is so important. I want you to understand in a "where the rubber meets the road" kind of way how to apply what you've learned with insights from my own leadership journey over the past four decades.

In this next section we will continue to dig into our motivation behind our leadership—not our methodology—because remember, unless the *why* behind your leading is right, all the *how* will not keep you on course. As you hear the echo of the theology we just uncovered in the previous section, we're going to get practical with four things:

- How to find your kind of smart,
- How to use that God-given voice,
- What to do with leadership pain,
- How to develop some grit to not quit.

Here's what I've found: If you are determined to learn, no one can stop you. Being a lifetime learner is one of the most powerful muscles you can develop; curious people are the smartest.

This is not a competition or a race. We all move at our own pace in our own lane.

And you should know the wisdom in these chapters is not for a sprint but for a marathon.

You're not doing this alone. I'll be walking with you page by page in this next section. I don't want to give you a theology lesson without telling you how to live it out.

If you haven't had anyone championing you in your gifts, I hope through this book you will feel seen and empowered with fresh confidence in what God has entrusted you with. In case no one's told you lately—or ever—I believe in you ... more importantly, so does God.

Okay, friend. Heart ready, pen in hand ... let's get moving on what to do with those tools you've been given.

I can't wait for you to pull them out and start using them.

## Chapter 8

# Find Your Own Kind of Smart

*Argue for your limitations and you get to keep them.*
—Elizabeth Gilbert

I was dressed to impress.

We weren't that many years into pastoring our church in the heart of the nation's capital when we began getting invitations to pray with congressional leaders from both sides of the aisle. Despite the level of power they possessed in the political arena, these leaders—when desperate—were simply looking for someone who could help them connect to God.

During this season, one of the congressmen Dennis and I regularly prayed with graciously invited me to participate in an informal panel he was hosting on the connection between church and state. He desired to emphasize the importance of praying for our leaders, as he had not only discovered a more intimate relationship with God but also sought to hear God's voice daily as we prayed with him.

I arrived to the panel in my white power suit with shoulder pads because, back then, shoulder pads made you look, well ... confident.

As I walked into the standing-room-only space that day, I was hoping that the suit would hide the roaring insecurities in my head. I hadn't slept in weeks and had a knot in the pit of my stomach as I found my seat. I was convinced I would say something stupid, as I had been known to do in the past. All my failed moments from my *entire* life played on repeat in my head.

To be honest, I couldn't believe I had been invited. Me—an inexperienced pastor struggling with how to lead—the only female on the panel. Nervous Nancy, trembling in a white power suit, sitting next to the other panel members who were all well-accomplished male leaders in the political and church arenas.

As the panel got underway, I was surprised at how many questions were aimed at me. Thirty years ago, my and Dennis's co-leadership was a novelty, and there was significant curiosity about how we led our church together. In a room dominated by male leadership, I was asked, "Are you submitted to your husband? Who gets the final say?" and "Who watches the kids and does the laundry?"

Crazy, right?

We went from praying for our leaders to talking about who was really leading the Pisani home and church. Despite my initial fears, I sensed the presence of God and felt confident about my responses and positive contributions. I was so grateful to God (and the shoulder pads!) for the outcome.

I neglected to tell you something significant. It just happened to be that "time of the month." To avoid a "white suit" kind of tragedy, I tried to quickly slip out to find a restroom. Before I could leave, I was stopped by a male congressional leader. He loved the discussion and wanted my card to invite Dennis and me to come and pray with him sometime.

I still can't believe what I did next.

Because I was trying to hurry up and "get outta Dodge" before my white suit exposed that I was a female in distress, I reached into my purse, but instead of handing him my business card, I handed him a pink sanitary pad.

Yep.

Right there in the palm of my hand was a little pink square of humiliation.

I was mortified.

As both of us stared at it, I jokingly suggested writing my name and number on it in a feeble attempt to rescue the moment.

Definitely *not* my most brilliant leadership moment.

My shoulder pads may have failed me.

I can laugh about it now. I've realized that God will use whatever is in your hand. Even the things you think you've failed at. Even your pink pad moments.

What I wish I'd known then is that I am smart and capable, not just in *spite of* my failures but *because of* them.

In fact, my willingness to use what was in the palm of my hand turned those failures and painful moments into my kind of smart as long as I chose to learn from them and didn't let fear shut them down.

At some point, I had to stop soothing my fears and flip the light on them to expose them.

And so do you.

## It Will Always Be Bigger Than Who You Are Now

In this chapter, I want to help you find your own kind of smart. Whether you are just starting out or you're a veteran, this is a lifelong journey of discovery. It's a wild adventure because you'll discover your entrustment will grow, and as you hone your gifts, the weight of what's in your hand will increase as well.

Entrustment multiplies and enhances your abilities.

Entitlement stunts the growth of your abilities.

And so, if we feel entitled to more before we start, we will bury our entrustment.

This chapter is essential in your leadership journey. You'll continually face the choice to flip the switch on the lies that try to define your story and embrace the entrustment in every new assignment God gives you.

I used to think someone would see me or discover me, and *they* would develop my entrustment for me, and then "a star would be born." What I've come to realize is that no one can do this for you. You must discover your entrustment no matter how small it appears now. You must be intentional about investing it in the places that appear to be hidden and anonymous, serving others with it. Along the way, you'll find fulfillment beyond what you could imagine.

Even though I have been serving God for over forty years, I am constantly and daily leaning into the entrustment God has for me in *this* moment. Every season has its own battles that tell you "You can't" to keep you from the fresh discovery of what God has beautifully gifted you with for right *now*.

Over the years, I've discovered the importance of consistently showing up and saying yes even when fear is loud. Those moments when I stepped out of my comfort zone often spurred the most significant growth and led me to discover what was in my hand.

> I used to think someone would see me or discover me, and *they* would develop my entrustment for me, and then "a star would be born."

I had to stop being defensive and protective of who I wasn't and become curious to discover who I could be.

Go back and read that again.

Some of us have been hyper-focused on who we're not, becoming masters of why we can't. But why not shift gears and lean into the boundless possibilities of who you could become as you surrender those fears?

This is essential for your calling as a follower of Jesus to effectively step into any leadership assignment God gives you.

Because the assignment will always be bigger than who you are now.

A few years ago, while speaking at a women's conference, I realized I was wearing two different sizes of the same shoe. I had bought a bigger size on sale for the future as I was between sizes. As crazy as this sounds, the revelation that they were different sizes didn't occur until I was awkwardly limping on the stage, as neither shoe fit properly. In that moment, God gently whispered that my situation mirrored my life: I no longer fit where I used to be, yet I felt intimidated by where he was leading me.

Many of you are ready for the bigger "shoe size" and are tired of hiding your gifts because insecurity and fear no longer fit you.

You're caught in the tension of not fitting where you once did yet not fully embracing the growth required for where he is leading you.

Now you're ready to find your kind of smart.

You, friend, are more gifted than you know and have been given gold that God wants to use.

We get to choose what we do with it.

## One Talent

Stories of how God multiplies entrustment by transforming graveyards into gardens are repeated throughout the Scriptures from Genesis to Revelation.

One of my all-time favorites is the parable of the talents in Matthew 25:14–29 because I can totally see myself in this story. It presents a beautiful picture of God and how he gives from his unlimited supply of wealth.

In the parable, a landowner entrusted his wealth to three of his servants to manage according to their unique abilities. He gave each servant a different amount: five talents to the first servant, two talents to the second, and one talent to the third. The five- and two-talent servants invested their entrustment and multiplied it, earning a 100 percent return. But the third servant hid his one talent in the ground and earned nothing.

The landowner entrusted each of them with something tailored to their *abilities*. He didn't give the two-talent person five talents because they would have been overwhelmed as they didn't have the capacity to handle it yet.

God has already assessed what you can handle.

Thankfully, he doesn't overwhelm us with the weight of an entrustment and assignment we aren't ready for; he knows our capacity.

I didn't understand this for years, consistently feeling unqualified, like One Talent. Insecure in the shadows of Two Talents and Five Talents, I hid my talent, always feeling insufficient in comparison to their abilities. In my estimation, they were the cool people doing everything I dreamed of with more finances, connections, and favor, and living the easy-peasy life.

Not two brain cells short of smart like me.

What I missed in the story is One Talent wasn't condemned for starting out with a smaller amount, even though that's what the comparison soundtrack repeatedly said to me.

The problem was their *choice* to hide the one talent rather than put it to use by investing it to serve others.

The story said One Talent hid it for two reasons; the first was that they were afraid. I wonder if they were comparing their one talent to those of Two Talents and Five Talents.

Comparison will always make you miss what God has uniquely entrusted you with.

Honestly, it doesn't matter how gifted you are; we all do this! Just a five-minute scroll on TikTok or social media leads to thinking, *How could I ever do* _____? *I don't have enough* _____.

I think a scarcity mentality subtly crept into the talent story, and the posture of entrustment swiftly became a sense of entitlement for more.

Remember, entrustment multiplies only when you acknowledge *and use* those God-given abilities.

Entitlement stunts growth because you feel as if you are *owed* more before you start.

## The Real Battle

Maybe you don't realize there is a battle being waged over you as you read this. The Enemy wants to blind you to the truth that all your insecurities are the seedbeds for miracles. He's a thief who tries to steal, kill, and destroy what God has already given you—abundant possibilities for servant leadership in your spheres of influence because not one God-given ability is insignificant (John 10:10).

Perhaps you've allowed the battle to intimidate you and you've wanted to give up, thinking it should be easier. What I've learned and wish someone had told me is that the size and length of the battle is not to *intimidate* but to *indicate* the value of your gift.

Because all of hell knows that when you stop listening to the lies and truly recognize your worth in Christ and the inherent value of what he has entrusted to you, your leadership and influence will become agents of freedom in Christ to others.

Remember, Paul's words to Timothy still echo over you to "guard the good deposit that was entrusted to you" (2 Tim. 1:14). The value you place on something determines how much effort is needed to guard it. And if we have to *guard the entrustment*, as Paul encouraged Timothy to do, that means it has the potential to be stolen.

Guard the seedbed of those gifts and assignments God has entrusted you to steward. How we discover, cultivate, and steward that garden within and around us determines whether it flourishes or becomes a graveyard full of unused potential.

Don't feel as if you're the only one who faces these battles.

This is the battle over humanity. God's story is chock-full of every-day people who didn't feel ready when God called them. Despite their weaknesses, they said a simple yes. Regardless of background, gender, or socioeconomic status, kings, queens, slaves, prostitutes, orphans, liars, deceivers, fakers, and, yes, even an ass became instruments of God's song of redemption.

They faced a choice: embrace the stewardship of the God-given gardens—which often initially resembled graveyards of failure, fear, and insecurity—or let the perceived limitations of a one-talent entrustment define them.

We also face this same choice daily.

Remember: *As long as you argue for your limitations, you get to keep them.*

I'm convinced that our feelings of limitation and inadequacy stem from us not fully understanding our unique entrustment, rather than our actually being unqualified.

Here's one thing I discovered that you need to know.

Every battle with insecurity, fear, and comparison (Hello … even writing this book!), I now see as an indicator, not an intimidator.

This is crucial for you to understand.

The slight shift in perspective that comes from asking the simple question "What is this (fear, failure, battle, obstacle) indicating?" will change how you approach everything in life.

The battle for what you've been entrusted with not only aims to steal all God can make possible through you but also to distract you from nurturing a deeper relationship with the One who has given you his gifts and authority to steward.

Too often we are like One Talent, allowing the size of the gift to change our view of God, the Entrustor. When asked why she hid the gift, she responded she was afraid, thinking the master overly demanding.

How you see your ability and, even more importantly, how you see God always determines the outcome. Your perspective either builds your potential or hinders it.

I've learned that 90 percent of the time, you'll likely feel inadequate for the tasks God assigns you to steward. He will place you in situations larger than your abilities—ones that necessitate leaning on him to transform the impossible into the possible. His desire is that you follow him, and your relationship and faith in him deepens in the process. He is not demanding or aloof. He is for you, loves you, and knows the *process* is an incubator for those gifts that transform *you*. The entrustment is in a seed form to begin with. The only way to develop and grow it is to use it and be willing to make mistakes along the way.

When you discover that any failure in life is an indicator of your untapped potential, you won't let it stop you, but you'll learn to reframe it.

## The Fear of Failure

Sara Blakely knew about failure and fear.

Does her name sound familiar to you? Maybe not, but I'm sure you'll recognize what she produced ... Spanx.

Beautiful, miraculous Spanx.

Who isn't grateful for Spanx, especially those of us with seasons of extra "fluff" in January after bingeing Christmas cookies in December?

Sara always wanted to be a trial lawyer like her father. But after two failed attempts at trying to score high enough on the Law School Admission Test (LSAT) to be admitted to law school, Sara wandered from one job to the next in seasons that didn't seem to have any purpose or direction. After seven years of selling fax machines, Sara experienced a pivotal moment. Seeking to enhance her appearance in fitted white pants, she cut the feet out of a pair of control pantyhose to enjoy the slimming effects while wearing sandals. When she saw how good she looked, she realized this was her opportunity. It inspired her to create a unique type of shapewear: thin, comfortable, and invisible underclothes yet still able to perform the magic of a girdle. Thus Spanx was born.[1]

Despite having what felt like a one-talent gift and facing multiple failed starts, Sara maintains her father's insight on failure kept her going:

> When my brother and I were growing up, he would encourage us to fail. We'd sit around the dinner table, and he'd ask, "What did you guys fail at this week?" ... He knew that many people become paralyzed by the fear of failure, constantly afraid of what others will think if they don't do a great job and, as a result, take no risks.... I believe that defeat is life's way of nudging you and letting you know you're off course. There's always some hidden opportunity or lesson in each episode—a chance to build your character. Spanx wouldn't exist if I had aced the LSAT.[2]

Did you read that? Spanx wouldn't exist if she had aced the LSAT. Sara learned how to turn failure and what some might consider a lack of "smart" into discovering her gifts and abilities, which is what I want for you. Reframe failure as an indicator to uncover its potential, rather than letting it intimidate you and keep you from trying.

It's time to stop building memorials to our limitations and failures and reframe them so we can get moving with what God has gifted us to be.

C'mon, let's start digging up that entrustment you felt was safely hidden away, whether it's one-, two-, or five-talent abilities. Because investing your entrustment multiplies your capacity to handle more. What is God's response to the person who invests and uses the entrustment? "Well done, good and faithful servant! You have been faithful with a few things; *I will put you in charge of many things.* Come and share your master's happiness!" (Matt. 25:21).

Did you catch that?

When you faithfully invest and use your "small seed" ability, God multiplies it and then grants you authority over more.

Your capacity, servant leadership, and authority grow every time you push past comparison, fear, and failure. What felt like a one-talent ability multiplies because of the experience and insight you develop as you go, because you deepen your relationship with the Entrustor. And not only do you impact and touch the people around you, but God gets the glory because of what he does in you and through you. You become a bridge for others to find the love and grace of God when you say yes.

By the way, you should start before you feel ready.

Is it easy? Heck no.

Is it worth it? Always.

Let me set some expectations as we continue. This chapter is not about how to get noticed, nor is it about how to build a bigger platform. Because the "platform" you feel entitled to will never be your starting point.

Maybe one day your platform and visibility will increase, and maybe they won't.

Whether God has given you one, two, or five talents, it's not about the size of your platform. God is not looking at size; he's looking for your yes, even in the hidden places where no one sees you. It will always be about your heart motivation.

> **Your capacity, servant leadership, and authority grow every time you push past comparison, fear, and failure.**

You'll discover you're not doing this to be seen but for an audience of One.

When you know the One who loves you ...

When you know the One who most sees you ...

When you know the One who is applauding every attempt, even the imperfect ones ...

Then even a scared yes feels different.

Because your gifts were never meant to be hidden.

## Your Kind of Smart

I wonder how often Phoebe had to repeat the letter Paul wrote to the church in Rome to boost her confidence (as we looked at in chapter 6). As a woman, she pioneered what it looked like to follow Jesus, hone her entrustment, find her purpose, and live it as she watched this baby church come alive to the gifts God gave them to build the kingdom. I wonder if she felt ready for the assignment to carry Paul's letter to Rome or if she just said a scared yes. All I know is these words she was entrusted to carry still echo over you:

> So here's what I want you to do, God helping you: Take your everyday, ordinary life—your sleeping, eating, going-to-work, and walking-around life—and place it before God as an offering. Embracing what God does for you is the best thing you can do for him.... Readily recognize what he wants from you, and quickly respond to it.... God brings the best out of you, develops well-formed maturity in you. (Rom. 12:1–2 MSG)

> We have different gifts, according to the grace given to each of us. If your gift is prophesying, then prophesy in accordance with your faith; if it is serving, then serve; if it is teaching, then teach; if it is to encourage, then give encouragement; if it is giving, then give generously; if it is to lead, do it diligently; if it is to show mercy, do it cheerfully. (vv. 6–8)

Discovering and using your gifts is not a new concept; this is how the early church was built and how the kingdom of God spread like wildfire. Paul and Peter championed both genders finding and using their gifts: "Each of you should use whatever gift you have received to serve others, as faithful *stewards* of God's grace in its various forms" (1 Pet. 4:10).

This verse sounds like a repeat of what God said in Genesis, right? Where God gave Adam and Eve the authority to steward their entrustment (Gen. 1:28).

At the end of the day, this isn't about you. This is about the people around you who need that gift God's given you. You could possibly be the answer to someone else finding their significance.

When our four kids were still young, I felt a growing burden for the families in our church's neighborhood. It was heartbreaking to see the hardships many children faced as parents dealt with addiction, imprisonment, food insecurity, and just the everyday struggle to survive. Despite my doubt about my qualifications, my compassion for these families pushed me to override my own insecurities and reach out to them. It started small, but every Saturday my four kids (ranging in ages from nine months to thirteen years) and I, along with a few volunteers, knocked on doors, distributed food, and held a high-energy kids' program centered on Jesus. Weekly, we cleaned up the crack bags, needles, and trash to create a safe place for the kids to sit.

It wasn't always easy or comfortable, but I just kept saying yes because the stories we heard of how God multiplied our "not enough," our imperfect one talent, blew us away.

The impact was profound. Families embraced Jesus, found support, friendship, tutors, and mentors, and neighborhoods knew they were loved by us, a local church, and God—all because of a scared yes.

That one decision taught me skills I wouldn't have acquired otherwise. As the program grew, it molded me into a compassionate leader who began to understand the authority I had been given to steward in *this garden*.

There is no greater satisfaction than the satisfaction of using the unique experience, strengths, passions, and personality you've been entrusted with to encourage someone else. Every time you say yes to an opportunity to be used by God, it increases your leadership capacity and enlarges your world—there is no greater joy than doing what you were created for!

## Finding Your "Gloria"

The beautiful novel *Cutting for Stone* by Abraham Verghese tells the story of twin brothers who were orphaned after their mother's death. One of the brothers, Marion, goes to his mentor, Matron, and asks what he should do for a living. She responds by asking him what's the hardest thing he could possibly do. He wonders why it must be the hardest:

> Because, Marion, you are an instrument of God. Don't leave the instrument sitting in its case, my son. Play! Leave no part of your instrument unexplored. Why settle for "Three Blind Mice" when you can play the "Gloria"?

Marion quietly replies that he can't imagine playing "Gloria" by Bach. He's never played a string or wind instrument in his life; he can't even read music.

> "No, Marion," she [Matron] said, her gaze soft, reaching for me, her gnarled hands rough on my cheeks. "No, not Bach's 'Gloria.' Yours! Your 'Gloria' lives within you. The greatest sin is not finding it, ignoring what God made possible in you."[3]

Whew, I don't want *you* to ignore what God made possible in you either.

Here's how Paul told Timothy to find and hone his "Gloria" in the middle of one of his greatest battles in life: "I remind you to fan into flame the gift of God, which *is in you*" (2 Tim. 1:6).

This is your reminder: Fan into flame the gift of God. No one else can fan it besides you.

What failed attempts, fearful opportunities, obstacles, or "pink pad" moments are in your hand that are *indicators* of what God wants to use?

They all have the potential to become your "Gloria."

What have you kept buried, my friend?

What gift is still in its case, unplayed?

Or what did you once pick up but have forgotten to use or develop because life is busy or the pain and the hurt of rejection have shut it down?

We all need what you have been entrusted with.

The world is waiting to hear your "Gloria," no matter how out of tune it sounds at first. Because as you practice, it will begin to sound like the soundtrack you were created for. It will silence shame, it will shatter hell, and lies will lose their power. And the people whom you've been entrusted to influence will be inspired to rise up and dance with you. They will find their rhythm and footing in your song.

Your Creator loves the sound of every attempt, even if it looks like a failed one; your "Gloria" brings him joy when he sees you learning, discovering, and using what he created you for.

Play on, friend—we're all waiting to dance with you.

## Hineni

*Here I am, God. I surrender to you all my thoughts of insecurity and inabilities. Open my eyes to see the "Gloria" you have shaped me to play, my kind of smart, the gifts and strengths that you've entrusted to me at great cost. I choose to invest the talent and fan the flame.*

Take this moment to personalize your hineni prayer of surrender. In what areas do you need to commit to finding your kind of smart, and where do you need to start using what you've been entrusted with?

.......................................................................................................................

.......................................................................................................................

.......................................................................................................................

.......................................................................................................................

.......................................................................................................................

.......................................................................................................................

.......................................................................................................................

*I say yes to all you have for me. Hineni.*

# Going Further:
# Discovering Your Kind of Smart

Develop the practice of asking God to help you discover the gifts you've been given. I have found that in each transition in my life, he has been faithful to illuminate areas I've kept hidden because I didn't see the potential. Cultivating the practice of immersing yourself in God's story by reading the Bible and praying will grow your courage and strength. It will be a constant reminder that the Entrustor of gifts is always faithful to help you discover them. Don't discount the hard seasons; it was often amid the greatest struggles that I would discover my greatest abilities.

Here are some practical tools to discover the gold in you.

## Find What You've Been Entrusted With

Here are a few questions to ask yourself to discover your kind of smart:

1. What are my strengths? What am I gifted to do? What am I naturally passionate about and love to do? What are my natural abilities? What is my personality? (Do I like routine? Variety? Spontaneity? Am I an introvert, extrovert, or ambivert?)

2. What are my experiences (vocational, family, educational, spiritual, etc.)? All these things matter, and God uses them as a starting point.

3. Beginning with my current occupation or role (entrepreneur, ministry leader, student, lawyer, teacher, mother, nanny, retiree, etc.), how can I use my role in service to something bigger and greater than my paycheck or myself?

You'll find these simple questions can open your eyes to discover your kind of smart and bring awareness to remarkable opportunities right where you are.

Discovery is step one; step two is understanding how you process to enhance your God-given gifts, which better equips you to collaborate with a deeper understanding of others.

## Hone and Sharpen Your Gift: Personality Assessments

Personality tests are not meant to define or limit you, nor are they meant to be excuses for bad behavior. They are simply a new lens to see through.

Dennis and I found these tests to be significant in discovering what our gifts and strengths were and how God could use them as we led together. Although we shared the same goal of building the church, we sometimes faced tension regarding our individual approaches. Here are a few assessments that helped us identify our strengths (and weaknesses) and learn how to leverage them effectively with our staff and team for a more significant impact. (You can find all of these tests with a quick internet search for an in-depth look into each assessment.)

- Enneagram: Understanding your Enneagram type will enhance your self-awareness and leadership skills. This centuries-old personality system identifies nine fundamental types, each shaped by childhood experiences and driven by a distinct motivation, influencing thoughts, actions, and emotions. Moreover, it's an incredibly potent tool for fostering self-understanding and self-awareness.

- CliftonStrengths and CliftonStrengths for Leaders: These two assessments aim to uncover your natural thought processes, emotions, and behaviors. They will help you develop a personalized leadership style that aligns with your distinct strengths. Understanding your strengths will empower both you and your team by fostering excellence and mutual appreciation as you learn how to synchronize your strengths for greater impact.

- 16 Personalities: These assessments serve as a valuable tool in your self-discovery journey by shedding light on your motivation and identifying recurring patterns in your life. They facilitate the identification of personal traits that may have gone unnoticed, providing insights to enhance collaboration in relationships and your ability work effectively with others.

- The Six Types of Working Genius: Based on the book by author and leadership health pioneer Patrick Lencioni, this assessment helps you uncover what brings you the most joy and energy when you work. This will help you find places to use your strengths and abilities to build your organization so that you can avoid the work that leads to frustration and burnout.

## Find a Mentor

Books served as my mentors for years, as I filled notebooks with insights. Today, a wealth of online resources, from podcasts to sermons, are available to learn about and hone those God-given abilities. Remove limitations and become curious, learning from everyone, regardless of age or experience.

When you find a potential mentor, start by inquiring about their availability for a brief (fifteen to thirty minutes) focused conversation, sharing your questions beforehand. Most mentors have full lives, so this takes the pressure off. Offering to serve the mentor in some way can also lighten their load and create valuable learning opportunities. Don't be discouraged by someone's unavailability. God has the right mentor out there for you; keep searching until you find one.

## Use Your Gifts!

Start at your local church. Explore volunteer opportunities and express your interest in discovering your best-fit roles and your eagerness to learn. Be willing to serve wholeheartedly anywhere with humility; this is key to growing in your abilities. I've witnessed thousands discover their gifts while serving in the local church and community, which also sharpened their abilities in their workplaces and provided clarity on their life assignment.

## Become a Lifelong Learner

An essential factor to discovering and honing your leadership entrustment is cultivating the discipline of receiving feedback without being defensive. This is vital for personal growth. We all possess blind spots in our leadership, and creating safe spaces for these conversations fosters a posture of humility.

Consider furthering your academic education. While this may not be the ideal season, don't overlook opportunities that may arise in the future. I waited until my kids were grown, but when I did go, it was life-changing. Don't let the insecurity that you don't have the right kind of smart stop you; if I did it, so can you! If lack of finances is an issue, you can audit a class for free at most colleges. Do an online search to find out about free or low-cost courses available.

Discovering what God made possible in and through you is the adventure of a lifetime. Using these practical tools will get you moving. Even if you only take one step, it matters. Be so good and confident at what you do that nobody can ignore what you offer!

## Chapter 9

# Nobody Is Listening

*To speak is to sow; to listen is to reap.*

—Kurdish Proverb

In a world saturated with noise and words, perhaps we have lost the art of communication because it is overshadowed by our inability to truly listen. Quickly scrolling social media reveals divisive and defensive echo chambers that highlight the urgent need to rediscover this art once again.

For those of us in positions of influence and leadership, or anyone aspiring to be, mastering this art is essential to effectively communicating the "echo" from the lips of Jesus.

Perhaps our insecurity resounds loudly within the echo chambers of our own thoughts simply because we haven't learned this art. Maybe, like me, you have either wrestled with summoning the courage to speak up or got stuck in the downward spiral of overthinking when talking too much.

As a result, the potential of what God can make possible through us remains hidden.

I used to categorize people into two types: those with this gift and those (like me) without it. And I was content with that because it felt easier and safer to stay in that space. However, discovering the assurance of God's promise to Moses when he received his leadership assignment—"I will be with your mouth" (Ex. 4:12 NKJV)—challenged me to refine my communication as I recognized it as an essential God-given gift.

Not only was God present with Moses's mouth, but, thankfully, he is with ours as well. The key lies in mastering the art of wielding this tool effectively to breathe that resurrection life into others. But let's explore the backstory of God's promise to Moses as it provides a more profound understanding.

I wonder if Moses clearly remembered the moment. He'd been tending to his father-in-law's herds when he saw it.

A bush he had passed hundreds of times before was on fire.

In the middle of his ordinary routine, Moses looked up long enough to see the wonder in the wilderness where he was living.

God had ignited the *ordinary*.

Perhaps we can get so busy in the routine of life that we miss the wonder of God showing up when we least expect it. Our preoccupation with the mundane often causes us to miss the extraordinary. It was in *this* place that, "when the LORD saw that he [Moses] had gone over to look, God called to him from within the bush, 'Moses! Moses!'" (Ex. 3:4).

This moment was significant for Moses. God ignited the ordinary. Common ground became holy ground, and that changed everything.

I have to believe this holy moment gave meaning to Moses's life up until this point. From being given away by his Jewish mother to being adopted by Pharoah's daughter and growing up in a palace, his life was not your ordinary rags-to-riches story. His Hebrew heritage was tested daily in this pagan Egyptian household, until one day, a circumstance revealed the strength of his roots as he reacted to an Egyptian guard who was beating a Jewish slave. I wonder if, in that moment, he grasped the full weight of his actions—the motivation behind killing the guard and the necessity to flee the comfort of the palace to save his own life. He probably had no idea that despite it all, God would still pursue him, using those forty years in the desert to set him up for his next assignment.

You'll likely be familiar with Moses's response at this pivotal moment in his journey:

Hineni. "Here I am" (Ex. 3:4).

At this surrender, God began to clarify Moses's assignment to lead Israel out of the desert into the Promised Land. As you can imagine, Moses wasn't sure he was the guy for this job when he discovered what his "Here I am" was signing him up for.

God often asks us to do things that seem bigger than us in the middle of what we consider a setback, when our identity is being battled over the most. I love how God responded to Moses's concern about going back "home" to Egypt because he had lived in the palace and knew what he would face once he got there.

God said to tell them, "I AM has sent me to you" (Ex. 3:14).

God was saying, "I am whatever you need. Wherever you feel the scarcity of 'I am not _____,' I AM fills in where you're not enough. I will never ask you to do something without first putting the seeds of potential in you that will grow from not enough to more than enough with me."

As Moses continued to argue with God about what to do if no one believed him, claiming this plan wouldn't work, God responded with two key things you need to know for your leadership identity and God-given voice:

*"What is that in your hand?"* (Ex. 4:2).

God planned to use what was already in Moses's hand, a simple shepherd's staff representing his identity, as part of how he would lead *and* communicate. God would use that not only to defeat the Egyptians but to make a way through the barrier of the Red Sea. The staff would become a symbol of Moses's authority to lead as a shepherd for Israel. It's fascinating that Moses developed this aspect of leadership (shepherding) in the wilderness, not in Pharaoh's house. God would use Moses's years with Pharoah, yet his leadership identity emerged from what could initially appear as a setback in the wilderness. Perhaps we miss the holy moments of leadership formation because we don't see the significance of what appears to be a setback. We can feel trapped in dry, barren seasons, oblivious that they are often *setups* for our future assignments.

You may relate to Moses' response to God: "Master, please, I don't talk well.... I stutter and stammer" (Ex. 4:10 MSG). His insecurity was screaming; his handicap only more evident. Moses had said, "Yes, here I am. Hineni." And yet, even with his speech impediment, God wanted to use his voice. Not only is our leadership identity forged here, but so is our unique God-given voice.

*"I will be with your mouth."*

I think the story of Moses is significant to our leadership journey because of these two keys here. The first is that God uses who you are— your experiences, successes and failures, background, gender, race, all of it—to create a unique "voiceprint." And, second, no matter what kind of impediment you feel you have, just as he was for Moses, God will be with your mouth.

This echo from Jesus is resounding over you right now. You have a unique voice. But you can't lead or influence without knowing how to communicate. If God could use the voices of people like Moses, who had a speech impediment; Esther, who was an orphan; Rahab, who was a prostitute; Mary, who had *seven* demons cast out of her; and many others who didn't have it perfectly together, rest assured, he can use your voice.

Whether that means you need a little wisdom on what not to say or the courage to say it, this chapter is for you.

Words are powerful: they've started love stories and wars, caused pain and healed hearts, reconciled nations and races, created business opportunities, and offered an invitation to change the world. Each word is a container saturated with potential, and knowing how to use words effectively determines whether your echo brings light or shadow to those you influence.

But to communicate well, we have to start at ground zero: listening well.

## What's in Your Head?

A few years back, when our life was more hectic with raising children and serving our church in full-time ministry, my husband and I often missed important communication cues from each other because of our assumptions. One of the funniest moments was when he returned from an extended overseas trip. This was a longer trip than usual, and I decided to surprise him by picking him up from the airport. I was waiting in the car at the airport arrival terminal when he called to let me know he had landed and was looking for his ride. I loved his apparent delight in discovering I was the ride he was looking for. Yet our ensuing conversation went from pure delight to a bit of hilarious frustration as we both kept repeating the same question:

"Where are you?"

After conversing back and forth for about five minutes and feeling as if we weren't connecting, we realized he was not only at a different terminal but at a completely different airport! I obviously hadn't been paying attention and assumed he would land at the airport he normally used.

We laugh about this now, but there have been too many moments that my "stellar" communication skills left me waiting at the "wrong terminal" with my assumptions. I've learned through the years that you can't build relationships, much less leadership influence, based on assumptions.

The novelist Virginia Woolf once wrote, "Words ... are full of echoes, of memories, of associations.... They have been out and about, on people's lips, in their houses, in the streets, in the fields, for so many centuries."[1]

Misunderstanding the "echoes" attached to all communication means we miss the opportunity for conversational sensitivity, which is integral to active listening and leadership in any form. Regional dialects, personal interpretation, and euphemisms affect how we see, process, and communicate with the world around us more than we realize.

Understanding the context and original language of Scripture is important in our attempt to identify the echo God has been speaking over women from the beginning. It is equally important that we become students of communication so the echo the world hears from us is clear and impactful.

I have been challenged to be a better *student* of dialect to become a better *steward* of communication, rather than assuming others' logic and motivations resemble my own (which I often do in a nanosecond). Somehow, my brain is wired for this descent into assumption communication.

Take for example the "lively discussion" Dennis and I had one evening not too long ago. As ridiculous as it was, my assumptions were out in full force as I prejudged his intentions.

After a long day of work, Dennis opened the fridge and sighed.

"We don't have anything to eat."

My assumptions went into overdrive, and my internal dialogue began.

*I should have stocked the fridge with something we could eat!*

*Huge wife fail.*

*Are any of those leftovers still edible?*

*Why do we have so much cheese?*

*Dennis deserves so much more.*

As my defensive responses caused this discussion to continue to epic proportions, the reality was that Dennis was thinking that *he* should have stopped at the store on the way home. I had assumed I knew what he was thinking. One clarifying question could have changed the entire moment: "What are you hearing in your head right now?"

Your leadership and influence obviously pivot on how you communicate. And perhaps the echo over you to "Go tell ..." has been impacted, or, worse yet, silenced, simply because no one taught you the basics of communication.

The foundation of good communication lies in learning to listen well and asking clarifying questions.

## Spiritual Hospitality

If we are taking cues from our culture, nobody listens anymore. Social media is full of comments and opinions, but *listening* seems to be a lost art. We have lost the ability to hear.

Approximately forty-eight million Americans—around 15 percent of the population—experience physical hearing loss, and 65 percent of them are under the age of sixty-five.[2]

Whether we're experiencing hearing loss, or distractions, or holding on to preexisting biases—confirmation, expectation, or false beliefs—the brain compensates by functioning on assumptions. This natural inclination toward assumption creates the illusion of hearing, diminishing our curiosity and motivation to truly listen.[3]

Most of us are unaware that our brain anticipates what will be said, generating its own internal dialogue. Perhaps this epidemic of not listening is affecting every realm of our lives, including the strength of our entrusted influence.

One of my favorite episodes of *Friends* is when Ross buys a new couch and decides to carry it up to his apartment instead of paying a delivery fee. With the help of Rachel and Chandler, Ross tries to navigate the couch up the stairs by pivoting and screaming "pivot" over and over again. No matter how many times Ross yells, "Pivot!" Chandler has no idea what Ross is saying, which means the couch stays stuck in the stairwell.[4]

How many of us have "hearing loss" and need to slightly pivot how we communicate? We may err on the side of desiring others to hear what we know more than we want to listen. How many of our conversations have remained stuck in a "stairwell" going nowhere because of this?

Throughout my leadership journey, I have seen the entrustment of my gifts and strengths continue to stay stuck unless I listened well *first*, rather than trying to prove myself. Sometimes we can move through life somewhat mechanically, not realizing how much baggage we've picked up along the way, which has created our frameworks of assumption.

Uri Hasson, a neuroscientist, did an "fMRI experiment in his Princeton lab that showed the mind-altering effects of prejudicial information."[5] He and his colleagues had two different groups of people listen to two versions of a story, with only one small detail changed. The difference was enough to alter the subjects' brain patterns depending on the "bias" they heard. What and how you hear from a previous bias will affect how you listen and will reshape your brain patterns. Kate Murphy, the author of *You're Not Listening: What You're Missing and Why It Matters*, maintains this is "an argument for listening to as many sources as possible to keep your brain as agile as possible. Otherwise, your brain becomes like a car that's not firing on all cylinders ... wasting its full capacity."[6]

So, if we are to be effective echoers, we need to expand who we listen to. To lead well, we need to pay attention to what others are truly saying, even if it's not what we are used to or even our preference. We have to drop the biases that keep us stuck in false assumptions.

I am sure you have experienced talking to someone who looked as if they were listening by nodding along, but in reality, they weren't *listening*, they were only *hearing*.

Here is why listening is integral to communication.

Researchers in psychology and sociology have discovered there is an epidemic of loneliness in the United States, which many are calling a public health crisis.[7] They say this feeling of being disconnected affects a person's longevity, and it is as serious a health issue as obesity and alcoholism combined, causing an increase in potential heart disease, dementia, and loss of healthy immune function. If social connection because of technology and social media has increased, why is there also an increase in loneliness and disconnection?

Perhaps we are *hearing* but not *listening*. According to Murphy, the difference is that "hearing is passive. Listening is active."[8]

As a mom raising four lively, energetic kids, I had a propensity for being a professional "multitasking hearer." Do any other mamas know what I mean, especially at the bewitching hours between dinner and bedtime? I wasn't really listening but rather distracted by the pull of everything and everybody demanding my attention. I would nod and say, "Yes, tell me more." But my kids discovered early on that when I repeated their question verbatim as my answer, I wasn't really listening. My lack of attention has become a part of our family's inside jokes as they have told me they learned the best way to get an extra dessert, money, or the keys to the car was to ask me when I was in multitasking hearer mode!

Such behavior is inherent in our human nature. Even James found it necessary to impart the wisdom about listening to the early church, advising them in a letter to "be quick to listen, slow to speak" (James 1:19).

I think I have done just the opposite. Insecurity had me over-speaking to defend, justify, or prove what I knew. Listening often took a back seat. However, the secret to effective communication lies in placing greater value on the person you are communicating with to seek understanding and connection with them rather than on the need to be heard. But listening isn't always easy. The author and theologian Henri Nouwen sums it up best:

> To listen is very hard, because it asks of us so much interior stability that we no longer need to prove ourselves by speeches, arguments, statements, or declarations. True listeners no longer have an inner need to make their presence known. They are free to receive, to welcome, to accept.

> Listening is much more than allowing another to talk while waiting for a chance to respond. Listening is paying full attention to others and welcoming them into our very beings. The beauty of listening is that those who are listened to start feeling accepted, start taking their words more seriously and discovering their true selves. Listening is a form of spiritual hospitality by which you invite strangers to become friends.[9]

Doesn't this look like the difference between entrusted and entitled communication? With entitled communication, you feel a need to prove what you know and make sure you're seen and heard. Yet entrusted communication serves the other person with a form of spiritual hospitality, accepting them by listening. The entitled influencer walks into a room and says, "Here I am!" but the entrusted influencer walks in and says, "There you are!"

I once heard a story of a woman who met with British Prime Minister William Gladstone and his then political enemy Benjamin Disraeli sometime in the 1880s. When the press asked her whose company she enjoyed the most, she responded, "When I left the dining room after sitting next to Gladstone, I thought he was the cleverest man in England. But when I sat next to Disraeli, I left feeling that I was the cleverest woman!"[10]

## Listening and Asking

Being more intentional about listening includes knowing the right questions to ask.

Obviously, if we want to learn communication skills, we need to be a student of Jesus and his powerful communication. His words were weighted with love, grace, *and* truth, and the impact of his life and words are still transforming humanity.

I want to be that kind of echo ... how about you?

As I began to study Jesus' communication, I was amazed to discover that Jesus asked more questions than he was asked. As we learned in chapter 7, the Gospels reveal he was asked 183 questions, yet *he asked over 300!*[11]

Wait a minute. Jesus already knew the answers. In fact, he *was* the answer himself. But he led by using the art of asking questions?

Yes, perhaps we have again been oblivious to the obvious.

This habit of asking questions didn't just start when he was thirty and beginning his ministry. No, this started early in his life. He was just twelve when Mary and Joseph lost track of him on a pilgrimage to Jerusalem.

After Mary and Joseph retraced their steps and found Jesus, he was "in the temple courts, sitting among the teachers, *listening to them* and *asking them questions*. Everyone who heard him was amazed at his understanding and his answers" (Luke 2:46–47).

Some of God's first recorded words to Adam and Eve were phrased as a question: "Where are you?" (Gen. 3:9). God didn't need the answer from Adam; Adam needed the question from God. It was a recalibration for Adam to take account of where he was.

Some of the first recorded words of Jesus were in the form of a question, "What are you looking for?" (John 1:38 CEB). His first question wasn't addressing sin, faults, or brokenness; there was no condemnation or accusation attached to it.

Each question Jesus asked served a distinct purpose in leading to a unique outcome. Some seemed elementary and uncomplicated. Others were rhetorical in nature or were left open-ended on purpose, meant to make us ponder and wrestle with what he was asking.

While I love asking questions, I never realized the significance of *what* I ask—I am thinking I need to change up my question-asking game!

How about you?

Jesus showed curiosity not because he needed more knowledge but because he knew what scientists are now confirming. Handing someone a solution can often become surface knowledge that is forgotten in the long run. But when you ask someone a question, by engaging them in the conversation, their brain begins firing on all cylinders, and the answer they discover is one that has the potential to shape the way they live. When this Rabbi asked questions, people felt valued, seen, and heard.

Questions serve as catalysts, propelling our brains to engage, change, and be open to gain fresh insights.[12] "Questions are sometimes seen as spades that help to unearth buried truths; or flashlights that, in the words of Dan Rothstein of the Right Question Institute, 'shine a light on where you need to go.'"[13] This concept, called neuroplasticity, simply means the brain isn't fixed like a machine. If it were, we'd forever be bound to old thoughts and incapable of changing our ways.[14] However, neuroplasticity enables our brains to physically adapt for creativity and learning. This means that neurons can relocate within our brains as we learn.

Asking questions instead of supplying answers fully engages the entire brain. As it reflects on potential answers, it draws upon intelligence from all corners, leading to greater insights than simply receiving pre-set solutions. This creates the formation of new neuronal connections that encourage the brain to seek solutions. Curiosity and the promise of fresh insights ignite the brain, driving it to explore multiple avenues for finding answers.[15] The person receiving the question gets motivated to action.

In addition to asking questions, Jesus also taught deep truths through stories, parables, and the way he lived. Yet let's not miss the point that the stories, the truths he spoke, and the questions he posed were meant to indelibly mark us. His questions weren't intended to elicit a how-to list of moral codes, "but were to reposition you, make you own your unconscious biases, break you out of your dualistic mind, challenge your image of God or the world, or present new creative possibilities."[16] They were profound questions, unsettling, ones that would recalibrate, realign, and invite transformation. Like any great rabbi, Jesus taught his disciples using the technique of asking questions to soften their stony hearts and break through their narrow minds, opening them up to the meaning of life and the mystery of God.

These same questions he asked over two thousand years ago still echo over us. In fact, you could practice by using a few of Jesus' questions.

Perhaps one of his most beautiful questions in the Gospels is also the one he frequently asked: "What do you want me to do for you?" (Matt. 20:32; Mark 10:36, 51; Luke 18:41). This question and all his others are fascinating because not only do they indicate his servant-leadership posture, but they also reveal his passion for serving others.

And how we answer his questions reveals our hearts as well.

Whew. This question alone—"What do you want me to do for you?"—is enough to change your world.

Here are a few more questions to use for personal reflection or in conversation with others:

> "What [or whom] are you looking for?" (John 1:38 CEB)
>
> "Who do you say I am?" (Matt. 16:15; Mark 8:29; Luke 9:20)
>
> "What are you thinking in your hearts?" (Luke 5:22 NABRE)
>
> "Why do you notice the splinter in your brother's eye, but do not perceive the wooden beam in

your own eye?" (Matt. 7:3 NABRE; see also Luke
6:41)

"Why are you anxious about clothes?" (Matt. 6:28
NABRE)

"Do you believe that I can do this?" (Matt. 9:28
CSB)

"Why are you so afraid? Do you still have no
faith?" (Mark 4:40)

"Will you really lay down your life for me?" (John
13:38)

"Do you understand what I have done for you?"
(John 13:12)

Hone your listening skills and your question-asking skills, and
build your toolbox.

As you grow in your leadership and influence, you'll discover that
people will begin to look to you for answers and solutions. Using your
expertise to guide is a gift, but weaving that knowledge into asking
insightful questions and then listening—not merely hearing—brings
transformation.

Management consultant and author John Hagel III, describing
the role of a leader, says:

> Leaders should ask powerful and inspiring ques-
> tions, convey that they don't have the answers, and
> solicit others' help to find them.... Research has
> shown that expressing vulnerability and asking for

> help is a strong signal to others that you are trusting,
> and you're more likely to be trusted in return.[17]

The art of communication isn't about trying to be the smartest person in the room; it's about listening attentively and asking insightful questions. You'll cultivate trust and foster growth for those you lead when you do.

## Confidence in Who, Not What

Like Moses in the desert, you've got to start somewhere.

We all do.

Even if you don't feel you have your communication tools sharpened yet.

We all need what your unique voiceprint echoes. Here's the good news: None of us are smart enough or good enough to get there without God's help. There are no limits to what God can do through you if you are living that hineni life.

I have so many stories of starting, trying, and failing, whether in one-on-one conversations or with a mic in my hands. But I've chosen to grow and keep trying.

Because understanding the art of communication as you influence as a leader is crucial.

I hope the wisdom in this chapter serves as a foundation for you to better navigate healthy communication and lead with excellence.

Practicing active listening, avoiding assumptions, and mastering the art of asking insightful questions lays the foundation for becoming a trusted leader who communicates confidently.

Don't diminish the small steps you take on your journey; remember, this isn't about becoming an overnight wonder but consistently staying curious to grow.

As you continue to excavate the treasure of who you are, let me encourage you to build your confidence by embracing who God knows you to be. Don't measure your confidence by your past failures or even by your perception of others' opinions about you. It's not *what* you put your confidence in but *who*.

> You serve as a voice for those who have yet to find their own. Together, we become a choir of resurrection that destroys the lies of the Enemy and infuses our world with hope and life.

Just as God reminded Moses, "I will be with your mouth" (Ex. 4:12 NKJV), he will be with yours. Although you've encountered this repeatedly throughout this book, the profound words from Jesus, "Go tell," resonate over you at this moment. Since he's entrusted you with a voice and instructed you to speak resurrection, it's time to start practicing.

Don't wait for tomorrow or next week. Ask God for opportunities daily—listen for his voice.

And even if your voice sounds timid to begin with, don't stop.

You'll have some failed attempts, but don't stop.

I wished I hadn't waited so long to intentionally amplify the echo of God's voice so that it resonated louder than any perceived limitation or insecurity I felt.

You serve as a voice for those who have yet to find their own. Together, we become a choir of resurrection that destroys the lies of the Enemy and infuses our world with hope and life.

Speak up, friend. We all need to hear your unique voice.

## Hineni

*Here I am, Lord. I give you my limitations, fears, and soundtrack of failed attempts. I hear the echo and choose to let you use my voice. Today I declare resurrection over my life, relationships, family, co-workers, business, and ministry. I want to hear your voice speaking to me.*

Take this moment to personalize your hineni prayer of surrender. Where do you need to be sensitive to hear the voice of God and commit to start speaking resurrection over others?

*I say yes to all you have for me. Hineni.*

# Going Further:
# Life Hacks for Better Listening

Honing your listening and question-asking skills will set you up as a trusted leader. For those of you, like me, who appreciate a summary or life hacks, here are few pointers for communicating well:

- Every day, genuinely build someone up. Put their insecurities to rest. Remind them of their worth.

- Repeat what you think someone said to make sure you're actively listening and not just hearing.

- Become an expert on your strengths, then stay in your lane. You're not supposed to be an expert on everything.

- Discover your weaknesses and triggers not to condemn yourself but to help you recognize who you should surround yourself with. Find people who are strong where you're weak.

- Lead with encouragement by becoming an expert on others' strengths, not their weaknesses. The more you see Jesus in others, the more they see Jesus in you.

- Always remember that today you could be standing next to someone trying their best not to fall apart. Whatever you say, do it with kindness. Empathy goes a long way.

- Do your homework and come to the leadership table not just prepared but overprepared. Although there will be moments when you don't have time to prepare, don't make that a practice.

- Don't feel like you have to be the smartest person in the room. Good leaders ask great questions with vulnerability.

- When talking, get to the point quickly and give the bottom line. You can provide details later.

- Be known for your curiosity. You can learn something from everyone you meet.

- It's okay to be wrong. Humility with confidence goes a long way.

- Compliment people behind their back.

- Switch "I know" for "You're right!"

- Pay attention to your tone, pitch, and intensity. Self-awareness is the difference between talking *to* someone or *at* them. Asking for feedback on your tone from a trusted friend can be a game changer.

- If you're nervous, take a few calming breaths before speaking. Remember God is with your mouth.

- Finding your kind of smart and how you're wired will help you communicate better with your unique voice.

- Instead of asking, "Do you have any questions?" ask, "What questions do you have?"

- You don't have to yell to be heard.

- Don't tell someone to slow down. Instead, repeat what you thought they said, and then ask, "How can I help?"

- If you're talking to an introvert, giving them a nod encourages them to keep talking.
- Greet everyone with a smile and a hello.
- How to argue with someone who's not listening? Don't.
- Whatever you do, say it with kindness.
- Listen first, then talk.
- And finally, *don't be a Karen*.

# Chapter 10

# You'll Need More Than a Band-Aid for That

*I am not a theologian or a scholar, but I am very aware of the fact that pain is necessary to all of us. In my own life, I think I can honestly say that out of the deepest pain has come the strongest conviction of the presence of God and the love of God.*

—Elisabeth Elliot

Mornings often resembled a three-ring circus at our house when all the kids were younger. Although there were moments when I had it all together, I was not the super-organized, professional, handy-dandy, Pinterest mom. Working full-time, building our church, and raising four independent kids with a leadership bent—a.k.a. strong-willed and opinionated—always left me feeling as if I were just gasping for breath.

In the craziness of one of those mornings, our eldest came into the kitchen complaining that her ankle hurt. She had apparently twisted it at basketball practice the day before. Upon further investigation, I noticed there was an area that had been bleeding but was now oozing just a little. Being the mom who was always doing three things at the same time, as I yelled to everyone to grab their lunches and jackets, I applied Neosporin to the wound, put a Band-Aid on it, and sent her limping out the door.

Around midmorning, I received a call from the nurse's office.

"Mrs. Pisani, did you know you sent your daughter to school with a sprained ankle?"

Feeling like the worst mother on the planet, I wondered how I could have missed this. Perhaps my morning multitasking wasn't working?

"I had no idea," I said. "I thought it was just a surface wound."

"No, it's deeper than that, Mrs. Pisani," the nurse dryly responded. "You'll need more than a Band-Aid for that."

I wonder how many of us have been putting Band-Aids on wounds that are deeper than the surface, hoping the pain will go away?

Pain is a part of life, so it shouldn't be a surprise that if you're on the front lines of leadership influencing people, pain is part of the package. You'll be criticized for bad and good decisions; people will assume they know your heart's intent and motives when they don't. You'll carry the burdens of others, which means you will often feel their pain and loss longer than you should. Betrayal and just the everyday challenges common to leadership and influence can weigh on you. And you may often feel you are the only one experiencing this and isolate until the pain goes away.

But what if the pain is deeper than the surface?

It was for me. And it might be for you too.

On the surface, it looked like I was thriving in my leadership; our church was experiencing so many breakthroughs and miracles. Yet below the surface of success, my internal dialogue consistently echoed with fear, failure, insecurity, and unresolved hurt.

My deepest instinct was to hide it so no one could see what was happening on the inside. I thought for sure I was the only one struggling like this; the other leaders I looked up to seemed to have it all together, all the time. I was fine when everything was going smoothly, but whenever I encountered obstacles that triggered an unseen pain point, an internal battle would ensue.

Maybe, like me, you have been wearing Band-Aids to cover that leadership limp that is signaling something deeper.

How you view this hidden pain shapes your perspective of the garden God has placed you in and the one he's placed within you. What's essential to understand is you're not alone or unseen. You're significant and loved immensely by the One who called you—he desires more than mere survival for you. Knowing he wants you healthy and thriving silences the shame that wants to hide the pain.

Because you can't heal what you hide.

Here's what I wish someone had told me: Every gift of leadership and influence has a shadow side, what Peter Scazzero in *The Emotionally Healthy Leader* describes as "the accumulation of untamed emotions, less-than-pure motives, and thoughts that, while largely subconscious, strongly influence and shape your behaviors. It is the damaged but mostly hidden version of who you are."[1] It's the side of us we hide that we don't want anyone to know about. If other people really knew what we were feeling and thinking, we could lose impact, influence, and connection. So, we hide our unresolved pain and emotions in the "bushes" and become like Adam and Eve, letting our shame keep hidden the areas where God is actually the most present.

Whether you are just starting out on your leadership journey or are a veteran, this is a message you'll need to return to often because it's the age-old battle over your voice. The Enemy doesn't want you to hear the echo of grace and forgiveness from Jesus, and keeping this truth hidden can diminish not only the health of your soul but the tone, cadence, and richness of your voice and leadership authority.

Remember, you have resurrection in your mouth, and the power of that good news terrifies the Enemy. God will use that entrustment in whatever state you're in, but I've discovered he wants you healed and whole even more than he wants to use you. While we keep showing up and making sure everyone else has what they need—whether at church, work, or home—perhaps we need to pay attention to the internal soundtrack that only we can hear.

In other words, don't ignore the pain, because it's an indicator of areas that need healing.

Hiding it makes us feel safe sometimes, but never whole. Only a loving Father can make us feel seen, safe, and whole.

## Blind Spots

Over the last four decades, there were moments I missed key leadership blind spots because I was so busy ensuring everyone else was okay. I often failed to check on the health of my own heart. If you're in leadership, rest assured, you have a blind spot somewhere.

We all have them.

I don't want you to miss any blind spots in your leadership like I did, because nourishing your own soul is nonnegotiable in leadership.

Psychologists note that our current culture is not only grappling with a form of post-traumatic stress disorder (PTSD) but experiencing a mental health phenomenon known as *languishing*—often referred to as the middle child of mental health. This state describes individuals who are neither depressed nor flourishing. Stemming from the aftermath of the pandemic, many feel numb and in pain and are unsure of how to address it.[2]

This is a book on the heart motivation of leadership and influence. Being a healthy leader or influencer is not just about growing in our spiritual maturity; it's equally important to acknowledge the areas of your emotional life that you've kept hidden.

In case you missed that point, your emotional health is directly connected to your spiritual growth.

So annoying, right?

But if you don't heal from what hurt you, you'll bleed on those who didn't cut you.

Scazzero writes, "The emotionally unhealthy leader is someone who operates in a continuous state of emotional and spiritual deficit, lacking emotional maturity and a 'being with God' sufficient to sustain their 'doing for God.'"[3] He explains that emotionally unhealthy Christian leaders have deficiencies that overshadow both the spiritual and the emotional aspects of their lives because they lack *self-awareness*. They don't understand or pay attention to their own emotions, limitations, or vulnerabilities from their past or present and the effect these have on their influence. They become more skilled at and driven by giving *for* God than receiving *from* him.

In the evolving landscape of leadership and influence, we've all observed leaders who, rather than being vulnerable and authentic with their struggles, tried to hide aspects of their life that needed healing. It's incredibly painful to witness the impact on those they led. Our tendency to idolize surface-level success rather than address internal root systems concerns me.

There are far too many leaders limping from unresolved pain; I don't want you to be one of them.

So, here we go.

Take a deep breath; we're doing this together. I've been praying for you to see God's love and grace for you as an invitation that begins pouring health and hope into your soul.

## A Soil Check

Exercising entrusted influence and leadership, even when the fruitfulness of good things is being harvested, requires a regular check of the soil of your heart. Slowly but surely, weeds can sprout alongside those seeds of truth, eventually impacting what is produced in your life.

Again, the things that will be tested repeatedly in leadership are your heart motivation and emotional health. The influence entrusted to you by God is about loving people, but let's be honest, it's not always easy to lead and love people.

Sometimes, people can be a real pain in your blessed assurance. Because we want to help people, we can attract hurting people. And people who are hurting, well ... hurt people. And the unchecked hurt and pain we encounter in leading can potentially create a hard heart for self-protection.

But the pure, effective influence and ministry entrusted to us flows out of a *tender heart*. The problem is that without a tender heart, what began as a sincere ministry entrustment can become a skilled mechanical performance.

Perhaps you'll need more than a Band-Aid for that.

It's time to do a heart check to see if you've picked up a few things that obstruct what the God-given gifts planted in the soil of your heart can produce.

Wait a second. "How does this happen?" you ask. Or maybe you didn't ask, but let me tell you anyway ...

I don't know about you, but I like helping God out a little.

Like when he's not moving the way I think he should. Often, I don't even realize I am doing it, unaware I've stopped following Jesus and want to control the outcome.

At this stage of my life, I have grown weary of upholding the facade of "perfect leadership." I am convinced that vulnerably sharing my personal leadership challenges can inspire you to be transparent about yours too.

One morning, a number of years ago, I found myself at one of our staff meetings thinking, *What is wrong with these people?*

I didn't understand how I could have come into this staff meeting obsessed with how much I loved them and how grateful I was for them, only to have my frustration go from zero to one hundred so quickly. Within an hour, the love in the depth of my soul had changed to a desire to fire a few people—or at least let my unredeemed Sicilian side come out for just a few minutes. Not only had they not completed their responsibilities in a timely manner, but their responses to me sounded disrespectful and dishonoring.

I was fuming.

*Have we all forgotten we're on a mission for God and that people's lives are at stake? Why is nobody listening to me?*

I felt we were not just falling short of the vision God had given us but, in my estimation, failing at it. Not only because our summer outreach wouldn't achieve the excellence I anticipated, but mostly, if I'm honest, because I felt like I had somehow failed in my leadership. My appetite for perfection, coupled with my resentment toward those I felt were only putting in half the effort, fueled my frustration and insatiable need for approval.

The feeling of not being an effective leader was starting to become the story I would hear in my head; no matter how hard I tried, it was never quite "good enough."

After the meeting, our eldest daughter, who was our executive pastor at the time, pulled me aside. "Hey, Mom," she said calmly. "Maybe you didn't realize, but you weren't clear on what your expectations were for the staff and ..."

She stopped for a moment. I could tell she was weighing whether to keep going. She took a deep breath and continued, "You were a little intense. Don't forget the staff are all in to serve the vision for the church. They just need clarity."

"What do you mean I was 'a little intense'?" I shot back.

I didn't like hearing about a blind spot.

You can imagine how that conversation progressed. Because I didn't want to hear her feedback, I began defending my intensity with intensity. I felt justified in my irritation because our staff wasn't doing what we had asked them to and their failure to achieve the expectation would affect all of us. I have since become so grateful for that honest conversation because it began a journey of self-reflection and self-awareness that I needed.

I wish I could say this was the only blind spot in my four decades of leadership, but it wasn't and isn't. I don't write this chapter from a "you should" perspective because I have perfected this and all my roots are in soil that is 100 percent healthy. No, I write this from a "me too" perspective, as I am still doing heart checks in the areas in my life that can cause pain to others despite my best intentions not to.

I am writing this as a companion who is on the same journey.

## Shame Off You

Let me ask you before we move on: How is it with *your* soul?

What I know for sure is, as you read, your pride will try to hide those unhealed areas because vulnerability doesn't feel safe. I don't want it to take you as long as it took me to discover these things.

Shame will try to isolate you and tell you that not only did you fail, but *you are* the failure. As leaders, we can carry more shame than we'd like to admit. The challenge lies in our inability to find safe spaces to share the pain, which leads to isolation and self-protection. Remember, shame wants us to hide the areas where God is most present, which is why it is so destructive.

Let me say this over you as a spiritual mama and as someone who's been on the journey for a while: shame off you.

Some of you need to print this out and frame it. Shame has been like your needy BFF that just won't stop stalking you.

Shame off you.

> Shame is a lie, and *vulnerability is your superpower.* It's okay to not be okay, friend. You can't heal from something you deny is there to begin with.

Go ahead and say it out loud right now. Set it as an alarm on your phone that pops up several times a day. Change those neural pathways of a downward spiral and create some new ones so vulnerability and authenticity become your soundtrack of hope.

Just as it was present in the first garden, the same temptation to separate you from the goodness of God is present now. Shame is a lie, and *vulnerability is your superpower*. It's okay to not be okay, friend. You can't heal from something you deny is there to begin with.

Let's go "bare-naked lady," as my friend Lisa often says, which simply means let's get vulnerable and drop the defenses and excuses.

We determine whether to wield our wounds as weapons of self-defense or transform those healed wounds into wisdom for someone else's journey.

## The Heart Is a Garden, Not a Battlefield

Part of healing is reframing how you see the pain or difficulty you've walked through. My brilliant friend Dr. Anita Phillips has taught me so much in the last few years about being present and not ignoring my emotions. As a trauma therapist and mental health expert, she maintains in *The Garden Within: Where the War with Your Emotions Ends and Your Most Powerful Life Begins*:

> One of the lies we have been taught about emotion
> is that thoughts create feelings. That lie fuels the war
> against emotion and tells us that if we can use our
> thoughts to create feelings, we can use our thoughts
> to overthrow feelings. Neither is true, but based on
> that, so many sincere people of faith are living under

condemnation for feeling anxious or depressed. The world we live in too often equates emotion with weakness. My clients who are Christians arrive carrying that stigma *plus* the belief that their emotional state is also a spiritual failure because they haven't been able to fully renew their minds....

The relationship between your heart and your mind is the same as the relationship between soil and a plant. Just as the soil is there *before* the plant, feeling comes *before* thinking. Hearing that may be jarring; I understand. How often have you heard it said that your thoughts create your feelings? How many times have you tried to find peace by changing your thinking, only to have that fear or grief or anger fade temporarily and then return stronger than ever? So many have reached the point of despair, wondering why they can't think their way out of feeling. The explanation is simple. We weren't created that way.[4]

In other words, we have been taught emotions are bad, and if we really had the mind of Christ, we could control them. Emotions are not our adversaries to be suppressed, managed, or mastered. They are *God-given* and meant to be embraced for wholehearted well-being. In fact, they play an enormous role in our mental, physical, and spiritual health. A subtle shift in perspective—viewing the heart's soil as a garden awaiting cultivation for health rather than a battlefield—can profoundly alter everything. Drawing parallels with the parable of the soils (Matt. 13:1–23) to our hearts, Dr. Phillips emphasizes, "Your heart is a sacred seedbed."[5] She explains that, just as gardens will flourish in good soil, the abundance we desire in life is intricately linked to the condition of our hearts' soil.

God-given emotions—deep joy, compassion, anger, sadness, anxiety, fear—are a window into what is happening in our heart soil. Even the emotions that we would have considered negative have value, meant to indicate to us what needs to be addressed so the soil of our hearts will be healthy.

One of the most challenging seasons of leadership for me was navigating a church through the pandemic in Washington, DC. The overwhelming sense of loss, pain, betrayal, and powerlessness hit hard. Externally, we consistently projected faith, but beneath the surface, life felt like a train wreck ready to happen. Despite moments of feeling God's closeness, many times he seemed distant and silent.

As hard as I tried, I couldn't *think* my way out of what I was feeling with positive thoughts.

Despite my best efforts to ignore, repent, or change, this cycle of pain became a familiar part of my leadership limp, which continued to fuel an *unsustainable* leadership pace.

I knew I needed help. Admitting there is a problem is one thing, but taking the step to get help is crucial.

Through therapy, this moment became a sacred pivot point where God revealed neglected areas of my heart. I uncovered a performance-driven quest for approval, fueling fear, insecurity, and anger when I felt unheard. I realized God never intended for us to suppress or manage our emotions with just positive thinking; that approach wasn't working! Acknowledging emotions as signals of areas affected by unresolved pain revealed what was driving me at an unsustainable pace for "success."

The revelation that Jesus intimately understands our deepest emotions because he experienced them is life-changing. "For we have not an high priest which cannot be touched with the feeling of our infirmities; but was in all points tempted like as we are, *yet without sin*" (Heb. 4:15 KJV). This verse emphasizes that if having those feelings wasn't a sin for Jesus, then it's not a sin for us.[6]

As I chose to acknowledge these feelings, I discovered and dismantled false belief systems, which helped me find the freedom I had longed for my entire life.

One of the most impacting things I learned was the healthy (and biblical—hello, Lamentations!) practice of grieving loss. I had been taught that grieving indicated a lack of faith, never realizing how unhealthy that perspective was. In leadership, celebrating God's additions is vital, yet equally important is acknowledging the ungrieved losses.

Intentionally focusing on these three areas helped me process my grief over what I had lost in that season:

> I offered gratitude for what I loved most about the season before the loss.

> I acknowledged what I painfully missed due to the loss, and then surrendered it to God.

> With gratitude, I was ready to start dreaming big again by listing all the endless God possibilities for the future.

Over the course of several months, this process proved pivotal for reigniting soul-healthy dreaming again. And it is a practice I frequently revisit, recognizing that navigating loss is a natural part of being human.

Because we're all in different places in our journeys, our next steps will be unique. For some it may involve just acknowledging the pain; for others, it's moving beyond that to invite God into this space *and* perhaps seek professional help. (I offer guidance for potential next steps at the end of the chapter.)

Getting the help I needed was an invaluable game changer, equipping me with healthy belief systems to fuel the freedom I now feel.

Here's some seasoned advice from me: seek the help you need to experience the freedom God intends for you.

While our stories may differ, what I know for sure is at some point each of us will bear the weight of a leadership limp.

The key rests in our intentional choice of what *kind* of limp we lead with.

## Walking with a Limp: Genesis 25–33

I can only imagine what Jacob was thinking.

As he awaited the approaching reunion with his brother, Esau, the one he had deceived so long ago, surely a flood of apprehension overwhelmed him. The threat of Esau's vengeance lingered even years later, prompting Jacob to preemptively send numerous gifts before reconnecting as both an apology and a confirmation that his character had changed.

Perhaps alone with his thoughts for the first time in ages, Jacob reflected on the journey that had led him to this pivotal moment. The weight of his early days, marked by deceit and manipulation, must have loomed large as he remembered deceiving Esau out of his birthright and double blessing, taking them for himself. The vivid memory of fleeing his family home to save his life: Jacob, "the one who grasps" or the "deceiver," encountered God on his first night in a way that indelibly marked him. It was in this vulnerable state that he had a dream of a stairway to heaven with angels ascending and descending. In this moment, God could have chosen to condemn, correct, or force him to face immediate consequences. Yet God in his grace reminded Jacob of his inheritance with the unforgettable words, "I will not leave you until I have done what I have promised you" (Gen. 28:15).

God was with him, even in the moments when he was oblivious.

Jacob took the stone he'd used as a pillow and made a memorial to commemorate that sacred moment. Perhaps we've missed that the hard places we're resting our heads on, the stony ground that wants to keep us from heart-healthy rootedness, can actually be a portal to God's strength and presence.

Despite God's promise to be with him, Jacob's journey was far from easy. Even after leaving home, he endured over twenty years of deception at the hands of his father-in-law, Laban. Sometimes God's "with us" means he allows us to walk through hard places to reveal what needs surrender, healing, or change. It's God's gift to us—helping us navigate challenging seasons—so the weight of the promise doesn't crush us because our character isn't formed enough to handle it yet.

Now two decades later, as he was returning to his homeland, Jacob emerged transformed. It was here, as he was embarking on a new season, that God spoke anew in a dream that brought him full circle, recalling his first encounter and reaffirming the original promise:

> Then the angel of God said to me in the dream,
> "Jacob"; and I said, "Here I am [*Hineni*]." ... [The
> angel of God said,] "I am the God of Bethel, where
> you anointed a memorial stone, where you made a
> vow to Me; now arise, leave this land, and return to
> the land of your birth." (Gen. 31:11, 13 NASB)

I've found that every new season and transition requires a hineni. Because every hineni we say is simply a response to and recognition of God's hineni—"Here I am"—to us first, as a reassurance that he is always with us.

Jacob pondered how this hineni marked a transformative moment, remembering that first night away so long ago. The stone was a *memorial to the past then*, yet now it was an *altar of surrender* to where God was taking him.

God will often invite us to take that memorial to the pain of the past and transform it into an altar of surrender.

Jacob could still feel the stiffness in his hip from wrestling until sunrise with God; sometime during the night, God had touched his hip joint, dislocating it.

Wrestling with God transformed the way Jacob would walk and the pace he would keep for the rest of his life. He knew it was a moment that marked him with a limp—for the rest of his life—yet he was tenacious and wouldn't give up until God blessed him.

He was determined that this time the blessing would come from God and not from deception.

And God's response? "Your name will no longer be Jacob ... It will be Israel because you have struggled with God and with men and have prevailed" (Gen. 32:28 CSB). The blessing Jacob had been waiting for was a new identity and authority because he *let God prevail*.

Jacob's limp wasn't a result of God's discipline. It was a poignant reminder of an encounter—a lasting symbol of faith that he carried throughout his life. His identity, pace, and stride forever changed; no longer was he someone who needed to manipulate or control but someone who learned to lean on God as he limped.

Our hineni limp changes an unsustainable driven-to-succeed leadership pace to one we can thrive in at the pace of our surrender as we follow Jesus.

## And Joseph ...

Now as Jacob limped toward a long-awaited reconciliation with his brother, he redefined himself as Esau's servant—the heavy cloak of offense, grief, and failure slipped away, no longer tethering Jacob to those identities.

But the story doesn't end with Jacob.

While Jacob and Esau reconciled, his wife Leah and her sons and his wife Rachel *and Joseph* were present (Gen. 33:2).

These two little words "and Joseph" matter.

They matter because there were ingrained patterns of deception in Jacob's family of origin. His grandfather, Abraham, and father, Isaac, despite great accomplishments, both had their share of deceptive incidents (Gen. 12:10–20; 20:1–18; 26:7–11).

All of us can be affected by generational lies that have the potential to deceive us.

It's our choice. We can let them form our identity with a limp of unresolved pain or a hineni limp of surrender that writes a new story.

Joseph was integral to the story. He had a front-row seat to his father's response to Laban's deception and later observed him limp into reconciliation with his uncle, Esau.

You never know who is watching your limp.

Years later, Joseph—after being deceived, sold into slavery, and wrongly imprisoned—would declare to his brothers who betrayed him, "You intended to harm me, but God intended it for good" (50:20). Despite his hardships, he named his sons Manasseh, meaning "God has made me forget all my trouble," and Ephraim, meaning "God has made me fruitful in the land of my suffering" (41:51–53).

You never know how God will use your leadership limp to influence generations to come.

Acknowledging and surrendering that unresolved pain, doing the work to heal the soil of your heart, not only sets you free but also has a profound impact on those you influence.

You are extraordinary. The gifts you've been entrusted with by God can impact countless lives. The stories woven into your journey can heal and ignite hearts for generations, testifying to what God has done in and through you. You, like me, will discover the joy in the journey because he is with us and we've chosen to surrender to the healing process.

You get to choose which limp you're going to walk with.

The limp of unhealed pain.

Or the limp of a life that daily surrenders with a "Here I am, God" in response to God's hineni to us.

Entrusted leaders and influencers walk with a hineni limp.

They're "leaners."

Followers who have found their identity in their hineni.

Shame doesn't get the final word.

God gets the final say.
Be healed and whole.
Shame off you, my friend.

## Hineni

*Here I am, God. Meet me here. I choose to acknowledge the pain, fear, offense, and grief that I've clung to as a memorial to the past and turn it into an altar of surrender. Show me how to lead with the hineni limp and pace of surrender.*

Take this moment to personalize your hineni prayer of surrender. In what areas have you been putting Band-Aids on the pain that shame has kept hidden that you need to surrender?

................................................................................

................................................................................

................................................................................

................................................................................

................................................................................

................................................................................

................................................................................

................................................................................

*I say yes to all you have for me. Hineni.*

# Going Further:
# Walking toward Healing

I wrote this chapter to help bring awareness, knowing that it would leave you with questions about how to move toward healing. I've included a few suggestions here to help you take the next steps on your journey.

## Consider the Soil of Your Heart

Seek the Holy Spirit's guidance to reveal any overlooked areas that are causing you to limp in unresolved pain. Do the work of healing by being intentional to find resources. There are so many books, teachings, and podcasts available to guide you.

Here are a few books that have been helpful for me:

- *The Garden Within: Where the War with Your Emotions Ends and Your Most Powerful Life Begins* by Dr. Anita Phillips
- *The Emotionally Healthy Leader: How Transforming Your Inner Life Will Deeply Transform Your Church, Team, and the World* by Peter Scazzero
- *The Body Keeps the Score: Brain, Mind, and Body in the Healing of Trauma* by Bessel van der Kolk, MD
- *Unashamed: Drop the Baggage, Pick Up Your Freedom, Fulfill Your Destiny* by Christine Caine

- *Safe People: How to Find Relationships That Are Good for You and Avoid Those That Aren't* by Dr. Henry Cloud and Dr. John Townsend
- *Reframe Your Shame: Experience Freedom from What Holds You Back* by Irene Rollins

## Read the Bible

Paul's reminder to Timothy that "God has transmitted his very substance into every Scripture, for it is God-breathed" (2 Tim. 3:16 TPT) emphasizes that the Bible isn't mere words; it's God's story infused with his essence. Just as oxygen is vital for life, God's words are breath for wholehearted living. Reading God's words and then speaking them out loud daily over our lives inspires, guides, and transforms us (Rom. 12:2; Eph. 5:26).

The Bible is the only book where the Author is passionately in love with the reader.

I would encourage you to read Scripture daily until it becomes a habit you can't live without as you grow more in love with the Author.

Here are some tips for engaging with the Bible:

Choose a Bible (if you don't already have one) that you feel comfortable writing in—I love recording what God is speaking on the pages as I read.

The YouVersion, BibleGateway, and Bible Hub apps for your phone are a good place to start. You'll also find hundreds of Bible studies or reading plans there.

## Find a Therapist or Counselor

While most of us are motivated to get therapy when experiencing painful moments, I recommend it during every season. Wholehearted living isn't just defined by a lack of pain but by a consistent pursuit of health. Therapy will help you identify what needs to be healed, guiding you toward health. It took me years to seek counseling due to a false belief that only people who were "crazy" needed it, but I have found that counselors provide safe spaces where you can navigate healing. You may need to try several counselors until you find the right fit, but don't give up—the process is worth it.

## Find True Accountability

Be committed to finding a safe space where you can be truly vulnerable. When you start feeling isolated as a leader because of what you are struggling with, shame can set in. It is essential that you don't do life in isolation but find relationships in which you can be honest and genuine. I cannot stress this point enough: healthy leaders must have relationships where they can be vulnerable and authentic.

# Chapter 11

# Don't Quit: Why Grit Matters

*The thing that I would tell a younger version
of myself? That the struggle is the point.*

—Virgil Abloh

Amid the frenzy of the 1850s gold rush days, R. U. Darby's uncle fell prey to the alluring grip of "gold fever." Obsessed by the singular ambition to "dig and grow rich," Darby joined his uncle in securing investors for their venture, and they embarked on a westward journey to the promising lands of Colorado.

When the first car of ore was mined, the haul proved they had discovered one of the richest veins in Colorado! As they continued, though, the vein of gold ore disappeared. Their attempts continued to fail, so in total defeat they sold the machinery to a junk man for a few hundred dollars. But before he began digging, the junk man consulted a mining engineer, who explained that the project had failed due to the previous owners' lack of understanding fault lines. According to the expert, the vein could be found just three feet from where Darby and his uncle had stopped drilling! The junk man took millions of dollars in ore from the mine because he sought expert counsel before giving up.[1]

There's gold in you and all around you, friend.

Don't quit.

I am not sure why I have no issue with not quitting certain things, like the seven-layer, salted-caramel chocolate cake I had for dinner a few weeks ago or memories I should release. Yet in the heat of the battle, the concept of not quitting often feels insurmountable.

So let me repeat that just in case you wrestle the same way I do:

Don't quit.

Just like the junk man, who had no experience mining but called on someone who did, you might find that the gold in you and around you is just three feet away in the hardest place of bedrock.

I've discovered that no obstacle, battle, or mistake—even those of my own making due to my stupidity, inexperience, or lack of knowledge—is the end of the road. They aren't final; my journey isn't finished. Every single struggle is an opportunity to grow in wisdom, strength, and perspective to build my character. In other words, there is nothing you will walk through that God won't heal, restore, redeem, and use.

It's all about how you see it.

*How* you see *what* you see determines whether the challenge is a source of strength or weakness and whether you will develop the grit to keep going. Because at the end of the day, leadership and influence require a gritty persistence.

Sometimes we miss an opportunity God wants to entrust to us because it comes dressed like an obstacle. We expect Gucci opportunities: sparkly, easy assignments where everyone will see our gifts. But God may give us what looks like a thrift-store version of the opportunity: one that needs some work to get into shape. We can sometimes miss the value, but when you take what's been entrusted to you and work with the Designer, you'll discover he has made the opportunity *and you* into a masterpiece.

## Why the Obstacle in the Way *Is* the Way

A legend tells of a king who got tired of the people in his kingdom becoming lazy and entitled. So, he put a boulder in the main pathway and sat on the sidelines to see what would happen. Frustrated, he watched as many ignored the obstacle or tried halfheartedly and gave up; some even complained bitterly about the king for the inconvenience. Finally, a peasant came by. He was the least qualified in experience and talent, yet not turning from the obstacle, he strained in every way to move the rock until he realized he needed leverage. After going to find a large branch, he rolled the massive rock from the road, only to discover a purse underneath filled with gold and a note that read:

> The obstacle in the path becomes the path. Never forget, within every obstacle is an opportunity to improve our condition.[2]

Looking back, I've often given up too soon rather than look for the leverage I needed. At times, weary from the continual battle, I felt it was simply easier to opt for the path of least resistance. The unbridled fear of failure, a reluctance to bear the cost of persisting through the battle, and the uncertainty of when or if the struggle would end all played a role in my yielding to the pressure.

If we knew the expiration date on the battle, we could endure just about anything, but that's the issue: we often don't know.

I was the most vulnerable to giving up when I carried the weight of the outcome rather than the weight of obedience. Wanting to make sure my best efforts were effective, I would become frustrated when I didn't see the desired outcome I had been working so diligently toward. In our roles as leaders or influencers, it's crucial we bear the burden of obedience to what God is asking us to do, rather than try to control the outcomes. Following Jesus requires surrendering control over what he does with our yes in our leadership assignments. When we take on the weight of outcomes without him, we cease to follow Jesus and end up trying to help him lead. In other words, the only weight he's asked us to carry is the weight of obedience.

So annoying, right? Especially if you are addicted to achieving results from your planning and tireless efforts. But the grit to keep going comes out of obedience, even when the outcome looks different from what you hoped for.

> ## The only weight he's asked us to carry is the weight of obedience.

According to the Enneagram assessment, my leadership style is as a driver or challenger. I revel in the challenge and prioritize efficiency and getting things done in a timely manner. This works, unless God's timing doesn't align with mine. Then I can find myself unwittingly carrying the *burden of that outcome* because of my impatience to see immediate results, which means, if I'm not careful, I can overlook the priority of carrying the *burden of obedience* in waiting for God's timing. This frustration has often left me with the temptation to give up altogether, questioning the purpose of trying if I didn't have the "talent" to see the desired outcome in a timely manner.

What I didn't know early on was that my tenacity to stick to it gave me something far more valuable than my talent ever would.

## Why Grit Matters More Than Talent

In *Grit: The Power of Passion and Perseverance*, Angela Duckworth writes, "Without effort, your talent is nothing more than your unmet potential."[3] Duckworth discovered that it wasn't the size of a person's talent that predicted success in life but the amount of grit they were willing to apply. She maintains that "many of us, it seems, quit what we start far too early and far too often."[4]

Here's the thing: you can grow your grit every time you dust yourself off after rejection, failure, and disappointment, and stop idolizing talent over the significance of being gritty.

Get gritty, and don't let anyone else's seemingly "more than enough" stop you from using what you think is "not enough." I recently heard Jamie Kern Lima (founder of IT Cosmetics) say, "When you change your relationship with rejection you change your entire life."[5] It is the fear of rejection and failure that has us canceling ourselves before we even try.

Wolfgang Amadeus Mozart, Leonardo da Vinci, and Vincent van Gogh were not born artists, but rather they carried the *potential* for art. Only after hours and hours of gritty practice and overcoming obstacles were they able to produce masterpieces. In fact, van Gogh sold only one painting of the more than nine hundred he painted.[6] Good thing he didn't give up just because he didn't see the outcome he was hoping for.

Adam Grant, an organizational psychologist, writes about culture's infatuation with talent:

> In a world obsessed with innate talent, we assume the people with the most promise are the ones who stand out right away.... For every Mozart who makes a big splash early, there are multiple Bachs who ascend slowly and bloom late. They're not born with invisible superpowers; most of their gifts are home-grown or homemade. People who make major strides are rarely freaks of nature. They're usually freaks of nurture. Neglecting the impact of nurture has dire consequences.... We cling to our narrow comfort zones and miss out on broader possibilities.... We deprive the world of greater things.[7]

Let's not miss this: "Neglecting the impact of nurture has dire consequences." Eugene Peterson quotes Friedrich Nietzsche's description of grit: "The essential thing 'in heaven and earth' is ... that there should be *long obedience in the same direction*; there thereby results, and has always resulted in the long run, something which has made life worth living."[8]

"Long obedience in the same direction" sounds a bit daunting—and boring if I'm honest.

But that's only if you forget whom you're walking with.

Peterson likens this nurture of a long obedience to "spend[ing] our lives apprenticed to our master, Jesus." We are in a relationship with him, constantly growing and learning. Peterson continues to explain that we are "not in the academic setting of a schoolroom, *rather at the work site of a craftsman*. We do not acquire information about God but skills in faith."[9]

At the worksite of a craftsman.

Every challenge you navigate—past, present, and future—is really the worksite of the Craftsman-Creator. You're not alone; you walk with the One who loves you most, who invites you to take each step with him as he molds you and your entrusted gifts. Don't stop. He sees you as his masterpiece (Eph. 2:10 NLT).

Your true potential emerges through building your grit.

God is inviting us to live a gritty obedience.

And grit isn't just holding on passively till the battle passes.

It's not a "grin and bear it" kind of gritty. It's taking the time to grow your entrustment and hone it, one step a time. It's the daily practice of resurrection. When you understand resurrection is not just a noun (event) but a verb (a way of life), and a person (Jesus), you can keep going, being transformed by the work of resurrection in you.

Transformation happens by building intimacy with the One who loves you most in the hardest places that need the most life and resurrection.

This is what leading incarnationally is: letting Jesus shape us until we look, lead, sound, and act like him. At the end of the day, that's the goal, right?

In my experience, the deepest wellsprings of entrustment often emerge from the most challenging places.

However, I've found that in addition to finding your grit, moments of rest and fun are equally essential. Not to escape the hard places, but rather to breathe deeply, find comfort, and renew your strength for the battle.

As delightful as it sounds to sit in a lounge chair on a tropical beach while eating island delicacies and sipping tropical drinks, I won't build muscle if I stay there too long, avoiding the obstacles. The longer I sit there, the more muscle mass I lose, and my midsection begins to develop a fluffy layer ... or two.

Muscle, grit, and endurance are built by lifting weights to create resistance.

A five-hundred-thousand-pound metal airplane lifts off the ground because of an equal but opposite airflow. And so it is with you ... reframe failure, comparison, and insecurity as the resistance that will make you fly.

As I look back at the hard seasons in my life, they not only shaped my grit but also molded my character. Battles have a unique way of revealing hidden insights. The more difficulty I faced, the more compelled I was to listen to God, recognizing that the battle was often used to transform me.

Ultimately, my relationship with God deepened and became more intimate.

He was the gold.

He became the answer ... and my relationship with him was the prize I didn't even know I'd been longing for.

I also surrounded myself with "gritty" friends, ones who had battle scars, ones who kept telling me, "Rise up. Keep going. Don't quit." These friends prayed for me and stayed with me. They formed a safe circle whose words were and still are weighted with compassion and victory.

Take it from someone who's been on the journey a long time: don't allow comparison and jealousy to keep you from becoming friends with people you should be learning from. I found some of my most profound friendships when I shed comparison and jealousy, ceased judging others for their success, and consistently welcomed them into my world.

Because you're going to find life and strength from what you walk through, but it's made easier by finding gritty friends.

## A Wellspring of Opportunity

The sun was climbing into the sky on the day Hagar's world came to a standstill. Abraham had just awakened her and their son, Ishmael, from a deep sleep by handing her a bag that was already packed. As he stood before her, his face contorted with mixed emotions, he whispered in her ear the devastating news (Gen. 21).

She couldn't believe what she was hearing. Abraham explained that his wife, Sarah, had ordered Hagar and Ishmael to leave. Amid the heartbreak and turmoil roiling within, Hagar realized she would now be abandoned as a refugee, thrown into the unknown wilderness, because she was now an inconvenience.

The announcement was unexpected, and as she thought over the last weeks and years, the weight of the bag pressing on her shoulders matched the weight in her heart. Abraham's plan for them didn't seem to go further than the food and skin of water he packed for them as he sent them off into an unknown wilderness.

I can imagine her voice as a fragile whisper, as, almost unable to breathe, she said, "Abraham, Ishmael was Sarah's idea. She believed he might fulfill God's promise to you. For years, we've believed this; it wasn't till Isaac arrived that everything changed. Who will watch over us or sustain us now? You would do this to *your* son?"

Can you relate to Hagar?

Perhaps you have been doing what you thought you should be doing, but the outcome looks more like a dry wilderness than the oasis you thought you'd be living in. Maybe it was the job you didn't get, or the husband who didn't show up, or the constant ache from the betrayal of a family member, friend, or spouse. Maybe it's the business idea that failed or the resistance of not enough money or time to succeed. Or it could be the kids that you worry and pray the most for, or your fertility process that hasn't yet been fruitful. Whatever it is, the weight of the outcome is so heavy it's difficult to spot any glimmers of hope.

After Hagar wandered for days, her water ran out. Things had gone from bad to so bad that Hagar hid a dehydrated Ishmael under the shade of a bush. She sat a distance away and sobbed loudly because she couldn't bear to watch her beloved son die. Little did Hagar realize that this profound moment of desperation was, in fact, a pivotal crossroads in her journey. Her desperation transformed this wilderness into a sacred space where God was intimately present and listening:

> But God heard the boy crying, and the angel of God
> called to Hagar from heaven, "Hagar, what's wrong?
> Do not be afraid! God has heard the boy crying as
> he lies there. Go to him and comfort him, for I will
> make a great nation from his descendants." (Gen.
> 21:17–18 NLT)

God sees and hears you even when you feel as if you're alone in a wilderness—in the hardest and driest places. The Enemy wants you to feel isolated, but I want you to know your unrealized outcome doesn't determine your proximity to God. He is there in the most difficult circumstances whispering to you, *What looks wrong and hopeless is not; don't be afraid. I hear you and see you.*

God is there, watching over you.

He says, *I see the dream you've walked away from because it feels like it lacks the life and oxygen needed to keep it going. The battle is fierce, but know I am close when you feel the most dehydrated.*

But don't miss this: "Then God opened her eyes and she saw a well" (Gen. 21:19).

The well was there already. Hagar just hadn't seen it.

In your hardest place, where you want to give up the most, God's provision is already there. He wants you to see it so you can fill up and cross the desert with revived hope in your dream and calling.

But you must choose to see it and take a drink yourself. That's leadership and influence. Stop waiting for someone else to feed and sustain you. You determine, "I am not a quitter." Every battle, every desert, every mountaintop, every valley gives you the hard-earned grit and muscle to fly.

Shifting your question from "Why is this happening?" to "What do you want to show me?" opens your eyes to the opportunities in the obstacle and the gold that is around you and in you.

Perhaps we *have* been oblivious to the obvious.

Some wells are found only in the hardest places that require grit to survive. You don't know that you need the well until the only way to survive is to see the opportunity in the obstacle. It becomes the perfect opportunity. The dream you've been hiding under the "bush" at the brink of death is the one you nurture like a seed with water from the well you discover in the wilderness.

That's when your wilderness becomes a wellspring of opportunity.

When, like the Samaritan woman, you start drinking from the well of living water Jesus gives you ... guess what? What you've been entrusted with transforms into a wellspring of abundance for everyone God has called you to influence.

So that wilderness, that hard place, that place where you want to give up? Yeah, that place is a gift. You're going to find grit and gold and a well that you didn't even know was there. Because what grows the most in the wilderness is your faith and confidence in God.

So don't give up. There are people who need to drink from the well you discover in your wilderness place.

The obstacle in the way *is* the way.

## It Is Finished

Before we pray our hineni prayer, I want you to consider that the obstacle that feels overwhelming, filled with lies and telling you to quit, has already been sealed with a breakthrough from Jesus.

He is already in your future, having paid the price for you to over-come with his final words on the cross: "It is finished" (John 19:30).

Knowing this is the gold, the strength that gives you the grit to keep going.

Two thousand years ago, hanging on the cross—bleeding, beaten, experiencing the betrayal of those who once cheered for him now jeering at him and throwing accusations—Jesus faced a moment that would change the entire story of humanity, pivoting it toward redemption, healing, forgiveness, and restoration ...

And he began reciting a psalm that was traditionally sung on Passover.

I wonder if Jesus' last words were actually sung over humanity ...

"God, my God! Why would you abandon me now? Why do you remain distant ..." (Ps. 22:1–2 TPT).

If he was singing it, what did his voice sound like? I've heard some magnificent singers in my lifetime, but Jesus' voice?

I can only imagine the perfect pitch and tone, the depth, the range, and the resonance of his voice as it carried a sound of heaven mixed with the pain of humanity's sin in that moment, until the last words of the psalm ended with a strength and a victorious surrender as he took his last breath.

"It is finished" (Ps. 22:31 TPT).

Those words didn't just shatter glass. They shattered the chains of death that had a life grip on humanity. The earth shook, and in the temple the veil, as thick as a man's hand, was torn from top to bottom. From heaven to earth.

What all of humanity had waited for was finished.

That song still reverberates over you right now.

It is finished already in heaven—all you face now and will ever face in the future.

Don't quit, friend. "It is finished" is echoing over you.

Even if you can't see it yet, there's a well in your wilderness.

It's in you.

## Hineni

*Here I am, God. Breathe fresh life into me; guide me to see the well in my wilderness. I choose to not quit but to offer you fresh surrender.*

Take this moment to personalize your hineni prayer of surrender. Where has the pain of past failures or criticism made you want to quit? Where do you need to fix your gaze back on Jesus to see him as the treasure in the wilderness?

*I say yes to all you have for me. Hineni.*

# Going Further:
# Practice Digging Deep Wells

In his book *Outliers*, Malcolm Gladwell popularized the "10,000-hour rule." This simply means those who excel practice an average of 10,000 hours before becoming proficient or excellent at their area of expertise.[10] I agree—grit and practice cause us to hone our entrustment. But I've also discovered a few wells you can dig to help you develop some grittiness in the hardest of places. It's like weight training to keep you strong in any season you face.

## The Jesus Well

Although the importance of building your relationship with Jesus is Leadership 101, I have found that in the heat of battle, the first thing that often goes out the window is my daily time with him.

Guard it.

Your proximity to God determines what you see. Don't allow yourself to become more intimate with the battle and problem than you are with Jesus. Proximity to him reminds you that you're not alone. It gives you the weapons and tools to keep going. I've discovered that worship music is one of the most profound ways to magnify God above life's challenges. It not only helps you to discern God's presence but also enriches your intimacy with him. Choose worship songs that resonate with his character, and prioritize daily time to let them become the soundtrack to your journey through the wilderness.

## The Well of Gratefulness

In *One Thousand Gifts: A Dare to Live Fully Right Where You Are*, Ann Voskamp writes, "Thanksgiving ... always precedes the miracle."[11] This impactful insight transformed my perspective, reminding me that daily gratitude is a powerful tool. Not only is gratitude a weapon in my mouth, but it always turns my "not enough" into "more than enough" as it transforms a feeling of entitlement into a profound appreciation for what I have already been entrusted with.

Mental health experts have found that a daily practice of listing three to ten things you're grateful for releases serotonin and dopamine in your brain, promoting a sense of well-being. Paul understood what science is now confirming, as he wrote (from a Roman prison, chained to a guard!), "Do not be anxious about anything, but in every situation, by prayer and petition, with thanksgiving, present your requests to God. And the peace of God, which transcends all understanding, will guard your hearts and your minds in Christ Jesus" (Phil. 4:6–7). Including gratefulness in every situation and every petition to God shifts the worry to a presiding sense of peace that is beyond our understanding.

I can't stress enough the power of a daily gratefulness journal, even amid seasons when you don't feel grateful for anything. It shifts the weight off you and is a reminder that the One who loves you most carries you through. Digging this well daily until it becomes a habit is essential even before you encounter a wilderness season.

## The Well of Confidence

Confidence is an internal decision, not something others can bestow on you. While encouragement from others helps, relying solely on that can leave you battling insecurity. In the process of developing your entrustment, practicing and honing your gifts is essential, but you can become a master and still not feel the internal confidence needed for grit.

Hebrews 10:35 reminds us to not throw away our confidence because of its rich reward. None of us would throw away money or expensive jewelry, yet daily we discard our confidence! Intentionally find Bible verses that will infuse you with hope. Then take the time to declare them over yourself daily. Your confidence will grow as you discover your identity in Christ. I have done this for years, not only for myself but also for my kids. In fact, for my kids, we printed out those verses and declarations, framed them, and hung them on their walls. We wanted the first and last thing they saw every day to be what God said about them.

Be resolved to build your confidence daily, and you'll find your current battles will become your future confidence.

## The Well of Safe Circles

If your obstacles or wilderness has caused you to question your beliefs, you're not alone. Pain often prompts us to rethink what we believe. Many of us have undergone a season of wrestling with the truth we believe and live. And I am sorry if you've experienced hurt at the hands of a leader or, even worse, a church leader. I am truly sorry. Whatever label you put on this season, don't stop. You'll find your understanding and convictions will only become stronger and more anchored as your relationship with God deepens. Don't allow a messy season to lead you to give up on God or his church.

I have found that while you may want to isolate yourself, healthy *reconstruction* requires safe circles of friends, including those who have been on the journey longer than you.

Find some gritty friends who will walk with you, encourage you, and challenge you. For me this took time and intentionality. While I wanted these relationships to come easy and just be delivered by the UPS man, I had to pray, go find them, and keep reaching out. Eventually the gold and the grit in these relationships became the gifts of a lifetime.

You can't do life alone.

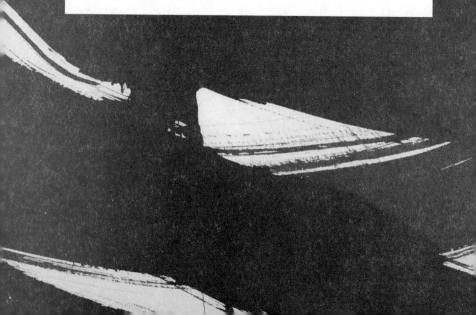

# Epilogue

I have loved every moment with you on this journey!

This marks a beginning for you, a pivotal moment. A crossroads where you determine how you'll apply what you've learned in your everyday life.

I have prayed that you would encounter Jesus in a fresh way and hear the echo of his voice as you read and that the weight of ink on these pages would mark you. My hope is that you have found truth and wisdom from the things I wished I had known that no one told me and that this book has become a field manual for you to navigate and use.

You, my friend, have been entrusted with leadership and influence.

I pray there's a new passion and confidence to uncover, refine, and serve with your God-given entrustment.

We need your unique voice.

In case you don't hear this often ... as a spiritual mama, I want to say I am so proud of you because of your commitment to utter a brave yes and take the next step.

You've chosen to be an entrusted leader and influencer, not an entitled one.

Well done.

But don't just take my word for it. Take his.

"Look at me. I stand at the door. I knock. If you hear me call and open the door, I'll come right in and sit down to supper with you. Conquerors will sit alongside me at the head table, just as I, having conquered, took the place of honor at the side of my Father. That's my gift to the conquerors!" (Rev. 3:20 MSG).

Every day Jesus stands at the door of your life, knocking with opportunities that we can miss because they often resemble a problem, a battle, a disappointment, or a failure. Even after all these years, I can still miss the opportunity because it is disguised as a problem!

"Anybody home?" he asks.

The moment we open the door, he immediately comes in and sits with us at his table. It's meant to feel intimate and personal, like a one-on-one with Jesus.

There are others at this table that perhaps you can't see who are cheering you on: those whose shoulders you stand on; those who know the value of the yes; those who have pioneered, failed, and then broken through; men and women who walk with a leadership limp.

Overcomers like you.

This verse (Rev. 3:20) is nestled into Christ's letters to seven different churches; this one was specifically to the church in Laodicea. Her trademark was that she had become super comfy and placed more value on prospering financially than on prospering spiritually. Her motto was "I need to protect my rights." She had become numb, neither hot nor cold ... nor in the pot nine days old.

Well, you get the picture.

She had lost her passion to overcome, go deeper, and push past the pain and hurt, and she was just stale and stagnant, settling for feeling *entitled* to a mediocre, no-risk life.

Forgetting what she'd been *entrusted* with.

Here's my final nugget of wisdom from four decades of experience: It will be a constant temptation to settle back and ignore the knock. Until soon, you don't hear it anymore.

The battles over your life and your voice are real. Remember John 10:10: "The thief comes only to steal and kill and destroy" what is of great value. And the Enemy of your soul knows the damage to his kingdom that will happen when you start practicing and speaking resurrection from an entrusted posture of leadership.

If you settle back, feeling entitled, you'll miss the table you were created to sit at.

There's a seat for you at Jesus' table, friend. No matter what you walk through in life, don't lose sight of the cost of the invitation and the fact that it's not just about you. It's about the others who will be impacted by your yes. The people who will find Jesus, the ones who are struggling because no one has encouraged them ... your yes will impact generations.

For a minute, imagine with me what this conqueror's table *could* look like in heaven. I think we often give up too soon because we've forgotten to live in the light of eternity and its impact. Keeping an eternal perspective gives meaning to the present moment.

The opulence and beauty will stretch endlessly, with one end of the table forever hidden from the other end because of the countless members of God's family sitting with you. Sisters, brothers, and generations of those who have overcome will be seated with you. Men and women from every nation, tongue, and tribe who have given their lives to overcome, even those who have been persecuted and martyred for their faith.

The ones whose shoulders we stand on.

Generations and generations of overcomers will be sitting at the table with Jesus.

The gratitude at the table will be palpable, as no one seated will be there by their own strength or talent but by the blood of the Lamb and his story of resurrection in their mouth (Rev. 12:11–12).

Our hearts will swell as we hear the overcomers' tales, many yet unheard because their overcoming wasn't on a large platform or in the spotlight but hidden in their daily walk of surrender. We'll hear how generations were impacted by their bold yes, and you'll understand more about the cost to be at this table. And then you will tell your story with the chorus of others, each giving glory to the Lamb for his sacrifice … and the waves and waves of gratitude we all feel will overwhelm us.

Gratitude for the Lamb.

And gratitude for the Father and the Holy Spirit, all three in a complete harmony of delight over humanity.

Finally seated in the presence of the One who called, empowered, and commissioned us and never once stopped loving us.

The celebration and the resounding shouts of joy from the thousands and thousands who found the One who loved them most as we all said yes through every season. Whether peaks or valleys, in times of darkness and scarcity or in abundance—saying yes even through the difficulties that wanted to stop us.

All the entrusted ones who've been limping with surrender will join in the chorus. They will echo the song of the Lamb from the second garden that silenced and shattered the power of the lie, the shame, and the curse from the first garden.

It is finished.

## Commissioning

My prayer is that as you follow the One who loves you most, your life will become a compass as you influence and lead others home.

After all, we are all walking in the light of eternity, with a costly entrustment to lead and influence others to join us as we follow him.

Entrusted with the journey, not entitled.

So, I end by echoing the commission from the Head of the church, Jesus.

Go tell.

Resurrection is in your mouth.

Be the compass he's called you to be.

You have a holy and sacred entrustment.

I believe in you, but even more importantly, so does he.

## Hineni

*Here I am, God. Use me. I wholeheartedly say yes to the entrustment and the assignment. I offer all my gifts and strengths, not for public recognition, but in obedience to your voice. Out of gratefulness for who you are and for your giving your life for me, I say thank you for your lavish love and grace. Draw me close to you. You are my joy, the One I am committed to live my life for ... forever.*

# Acknowledgments

In the beautiful tapestry of life, our stories our interwoven with the influence of countless others, enriching the fabric of who we are. This book is no exception. Throughout the years, the lives and stories of others have added wisdom, encouragement, and strength to my leadership journey. Here are a few I want to acknowledge:

Dennis, my husband and best friend, thank you for the consistent encouragement and nudge to see and use the potential my insecurity wanted to keep hidden. I have loved doing this leadership journey as we learned and pioneered together. Your unwavering support to give me space and time to pursue graduate school and write this book, alongside your continual prayer, steadfast faith, and profound wisdom, has been my rock ... you are truly my greatest gift.

Bethany, Alex, Jessica, Gabs, Colbey, and Evan, your invaluable insight and feedback as I wrestled with how to convey the message enriched the book immeasurably. Your constant encouragement and willingness to sacrifice time with your mama as I was immersed in writing mean the world to me. I am so proud of all of you and wrote this book with you in mind. You will always be the joy of my heart!

Mom and Dad, thank you for always believing in me. Your passion for learning, endless curiosity, and encouragement inspired me to further my education, laying the groundwork for this book. Paul and Michelle, more than siblings, you are deeply loved friends and invaluable prayer partners. I am so beyond grateful for you.

Dr. Leonard Sweet, I am deeply grateful for the impact you've had on my academic journey and for being a beloved mentor to me. You have transformed the way I see life and ministry with your profound wisdom and teaching in a season that I cherish. Thank you. Dr. Greg Borror, you made my DMin journey discernible and possible. This book is the by-product of the rich insight and wisdom you consistently added. Thank you.

Drs. Terry Crist, Scott Jones, and Jeremy DeWeerdt, my "older" brothers and colleagues, I am grateful for your constant encouragement and humor, without which I don't think I would have survived (or understood our assignments!) as we embarked on this academic journey together from our master's to DMin. You three, with your wives—Judith, Jen, and Mel—have become lifetime gifts whom I love dearly.

Dr. Melissa Archer and Dr. A. J. Swoboda, your classes during my master's program ignited a passion for this theology, spurred me to further my education, and were the nudge I needed to write a book on this subject. Thank you. Dr. Lynn Cohick, your trusted voice and wisdom were a beautiful compass as I wrote section 1; thank you. Emily Bradley, thanks for editing research papers and teaching me how to write in the process; I am forever grateful! Travis Thatcher, without *your* edits this book wouldn't have gotten to this stage! Thank you.

To my literary agent and friends, Esther Fedorkevich and Danielle Hale, thank you for seeing the need for a book on leadership for women. You consistently inspire me the way you lead in business.

Susan McPherson, Stephanie Bennett, Marianne Hering, and Esther Press, thank you for the unwavering encouragement that became the fuel to keep this book moving from a messy manuscript to a honed message that will impact generations.

Mark and Lora Batterson, you are dearly loved longtime friends "tilling the same soil" as pastors in the Washington DC Metro area but now are *our* pastors after our church became one with National Community Church. Thank you for believing in me as an author and for being deep wells of wisdom and encouragement.

Holly Wagner, my dear friend, thank you for being a "door holder" to use my voice and encouraging me to write a "smart book" on this subject. I love doing this season of life with you as we mentor younger women in leadership.

Julie Mullins, your friendship and constant encouragement for this book have been invaluable. Thank you for living this message. You inspire all of us with your humility and strength.

Lisa Jennett, your prayer, friendship, and prophetic sense have been one of the greatest treasures to me. Love you dearly and am grateful for who you are to our family.

Dr. Anita Phillips, your friendship and wisdom have been pure gold. Listening to you talk about the "garden within" has transformed much of how I see life. Love you deeply! Julie Mullins, your friendship and constant encouragement for this book have been invaluable. Thank you for living what this book is about. You inspire all of us with your grace and strength.

Christine Caine, my dearly loved friend, thanks for the nudge to write this book. It is your pioneering voice that has consistently challenged me to not settle for less than what God has ... I am so grateful.

Ann Voskamp, your words have always marked me, but our conversation over coffee in Paris inspired me deeply and was the wind I needed in my sails to write this book. Thank you.

Lisa Harper, your hunger for biblical literacy, and ability to communicate with humor and depth, make us yearn for it as well. Your friendship has been a source of encouragement and influence in my life. Thank you.

To the women who have pioneered the way, the ones on whose shoulders we all stand, so many (too many to mention here) who have mentored me from afar with their voices, challenged me with their courage, inspired me with their sacrifice and humility, thank you.

Most of all to God. You are magnificent in every way, especially in how your unceasing, unlimited love heals my heart and how you use the broken pieces of my life to inspire others. Thank you for taking a scared, insecure teenager on the journey of a lifetime and never giving up on me even when I wanted to give up. The rich relationship I have with you now is the prize I've always longed for.

# Notes

## Introduction

1. Gordon D. Fee, *Listening to the Spirit in the Text* (Grand Rapids, MI: Eerdmans, 2000), 3.

2. Patrick Lencioni, *The Motive: Why So Many Leaders Abdicate Their Most Important Responsibilities; A Leadership Fable* (Hoboken, NJ: John Wiley & Sons, 2020), 130.

## Chapter 1

1. John 19:30.

2. Mark 16:1.

3. John 20:13.

4. John 20:13.

5. John 20:15.

6. John 20:15.

7. John 20:16.

8. John 20:16.

9. John 20:17 NLT.

10. 2 Timothy 3:16–17.

11. Genesis 1:3.

## Chapter 3

1. Patrick Lencioni, *The Motive: Why So Many Leaders Abdicate Their Most Important Responsibilities; A Leadership Fable* (Hoboken, NJ: John Wiley & Sons, 2020), 131.

2. Lencioni, *The Motive*, 131.

3. Lencioni, 130.

4. "1904 Diego Rivera 'El Albañil' Oil Painting," *Antiques Roadshow*, PBS, 2018, www.pbs.org/wgbh/roadshow/season/17/corpus-christi-tx/appraisals/1904-diego -rivera-el-albanil-oil--201205A27.

5. Leonard Sweet, "Asynchronous Chat" (lecture, Portland Seminary, Portland, OR, March 31, 2021).

6. Bob Goff, *Live in Grace, Walk in Love: A 365-Day Journey* (Nashville: Nelson Books, 2019), 265.

## Chapter 4

1. A.W. Tozer, *The Knowledge of the Holy* (New York: Harper Collins, 1961), 2.

2. Dorothy L. Sayers, *Are Women Human?* (Grand Rapids, MI: William B. Eerdmans, 1971), 47.

3. Alice Mathews, *Gender Roles and the People of God: Rethinking What We Were Taught about Men and Women in the Church* (Grand Rapids, MI: Zondervan, 2017), 70.

4. H. Wayne House, *The Role of Women in Ministry Today* (Grand Rapids, MI: Baker, 1995), 21, 82, emphasis added.

5. Rob Dixon, *Together in Ministry: Women and Men in Flourishing Partnerships* (Downers Grove, IL: IVP Academic, 2021), 5.

6. Mary J. Evans, *Woman in the Bible: An Overview of All the Crucial Passages on Women's Roles* (Downers Grove, IL: InterVarsity Press, 1982), 45 (emphasis added).

7. Loren Cunningham and David Joel Hamilton, *Why Not Women? A Fresh Look at Scripture on Women in Missions, Ministry and Leadership*, with Janice Rogers (Seattle, WA: YWAM Publishing, 2000), 119.

8. Cunningham and Hamilton, *Why Not Women?*, 119.

9. Sharon Hodgin Gritz, *Paul, Women Teachers, and the Mother Goddess at Ephesus: A Study of 1 Timothy 2:9–15 in Light of the Religious and Cultural Milieu of the First Century* (Lanham, MD: University Press of America, 1991), 75.

10. Ronald W. Pierce, Cynthia Long Westfall, and Christa L. McKirland, eds., *Discovering Biblical Equality: Biblical, Theological, Cultural, and Practical Perspectives*, 3rd ed. (Downers Grove, IL: InterVarsity Press, 2021), 99.

11. Philip B. Payne, *Man and Woman, One in Christ: An Exegetical and Theological Study of Paul's Letters* (Grand Rapids, MI: Zondervan, 2009), 58.

12. Ben Witherington III, *Women and the Genesis of Christianity,* ed. Ann Witherington (Cambridge: Cambridge University Press, 1990), 78–80.

13. Craig Keener, "Women's Education and Public Speech in Antiquity," *JETS* 50, no. 4 (December 2007): 750.

14. David M. Scholer, "Writing and Literature: Greco-Roman," in *Dictionary of New Testament Background*, ed. Craig A. Evans and Stanley E. Porter (Downers Grove, IL: InterVarsity Press, 2000), 1283.

15. Kenneth E. Bailey, *Jesus through Middle Eastern Eyes: Cultural Studies in the Gospels* (Downers Grove, IL: InterVarsity Press, 2008), 193.

16. Kevin Giles, *What the Bible Actually Teaches on Women* (Eugene, OR: Cascade Books, 2018), 79.

17. Aída Besançon Spencer, *Beyond the Curse: Women Called to Ministry* (Grand Rapids, MI: Baker Academic, 1985), 60 (emphasis in original).

18. Philip B. Payne, *The Bible vs. Biblical Womanhood: How God's Word Consistently Affirms Gender Equality* (Grand Rapids, MI: Zondervan, 2023), 28.

19. Sandra Glahn, ed., *Vindicating the Vixens: Revisiting Sexualized, Vilified, and Marginalized Women of the Bible* (Grand Rapids, MI: Kregel Publications, 2017), chap. 12, Kindle.

20. James Strong, *Strong's Expanded Exhaustive Concordance of the Bible* (Nashville: Thomas Nelson, 2009), minister 1247, *diakoneo.*

21. Michael J. Wilkins, "Women in the Teaching and Example of Jesus," in *Women and Men in Ministry: A Complementary Perspective*, ed. Robert L. Saucy and Judith K. TenElshof (Chicago: Moody, 2001), 95, 97–8, 100.

22. Payne, *The Bible vs. Biblical Womanhood*, 29–30.

23. Payne, 30.

24. Pierce, Westfall, and McKirland, *Discovering Biblical Equality*, 101.

25. Matthew 4:20, 22; Mark 1:18, 20.

26. Dorothy A. Lee, *The Ministry of Women in the New Testament: Reclaiming the Biblical Vision for Church Leadership* (Grand Rapids, MI: Baker Academic, 2021), chap. 1, Kindle.

27. John Calvin, "Commentary on a Harmony of the Evangelists, Matthew, Mark, and Luke," vol. 3, in *Harmony of Matthew, Mark, Luke, John 1–11*, trans. William Pringle, Calvin's Commentaries, vol. 17 (reprint, Grand Rapids, MI: Baker, 2003), 329.

## Chapter 5

1. Megan Marples, "Decision Fatigue Drains You of Your Energy to Make Thoughtful Choices. Here's How to Get it Back," CNN, April 21, 2022, www.cnn .com/2022/04/21/health/decision-fatigue-solutions-wellness/index.html#.

2. Arjun Vijeth, "How Your Choices Can Shape Your Future—A Guide to Making Conscious Choices for Success," LinkedIn, April 16, 2023, www.linkedin.com /pulse/how-your-choices-can-shape-future-guide-making-conscious-vijeth.

3. Makoto Fujimura, *Art and Faith: A Theology of Making* (New Haven, CT: Yale University Press, 2020), 7.

4. Sue Edwards and Kelley Mathews, *40 Questions about Women in Ministry* (Grand Rapids, MI: Kregel Academic, 2022), 74–82.

5. Edwards and Mathews, *40 Questions about Women in Ministry*, 65–101.

6. Rebecca Merrill Groothuis, *Good News for Women: A Biblical Picture of Gender Equality* (Grand Rapids, MI: Baker Books, 1996), 137.

7. Sandra L. Richter, *The Epic of Eden: A Christian Entry into the Old Testament* (Downers Grove, IL: InterVarsity Press, 2008), 107.

8. John H. Walton, *The Lost World of Adam and Eve: Genesis 2–3 and the Human Origins Debate*, with a contribution by N. T. Wright (Downers Grove, IL: InterVarsity Press, 2015), 42.

9. Preston Sprinkle, "Does the Old Testament Dehumanize Women? Dr. Sandy Richter (Exiles 22 Talk + Q & A)," February 9, 2023, YouTube video, www.youtube .com/watch?v=AjnMM36QUjA.

10. Richter, *The Epic of Eden*, 170.

11. Frank E. Gaebelein, *The Expositor's Bible Commentary*, vol. 2 (Grand Rapids, MI: Zondervan, 1990), 2.

12. Charles M. Laymon, ed., *The Interpreter's One-Volume Commentary on the Bible* (Nashville: Abingdon Press, 1971), 4.

13. Bruce M. Metzger and Michael D. Coogan, eds., *The Oxford Companion to the Bible* (New York: Oxford University Press, 1993), 806.

14. James Swanson, *Dictionary of Biblical Languages with Semantic Domains: Hebrew* (Oak Harbor, WA: Logos Research Systems, 1997), 6949.

15. Edwards and Mathews, *40 Questions About Women in Ministry*, 92.

16. Exodus 18:4; Deuteronomy 33:7; Psalm 18:4; 20:2; 33:20; 70:5; 89:19; 115:9–11; 121:2; 124:8.

17. Edwards and Mathews, *40 Questions about Women in Ministry*, 92.

18. John H. Walton, *Genesis: The NIV Application Commentary* (Grand Rapids, MI: Zondervan, 2001), 175, 177.

19. R. David Freedman, "Woman, a Power Equal to Man: Translation of Woman a 'Fit Helpmate' for Man Is Questioned," *Biblical Archaeology Review* 9, no. 1 (January/February 1983): 58.

20. Walter C. Kaiser Jr., Peter H. Davids, F. F. Bruce, and Manfred T. Brauch, *Hard Sayings of the Bible* (Downers Grove, IL: InterVarsity Press, 1996), 94.

21. Freedman, "Woman, a Power Equal to Man," 58.

22. Sprinkle, "Does the Old Testament Dehumanize Women?"

23. Richter, *The Epic of Eden*, 106, emphasis in original.

24. Mignon R. Jacobs, *Gender, Power, and Persuasion: The Genesis Narratives and Contemporary Portraits* (Grand Rapids, MI: Baker Academic, 2007), 58–64.

25. Scot McKnight, *The Blue Parakeet: Rethinking How You Read the Bible*, 2nd ed. (Grand Rapids, MI: Zondervan, 2018), 216.

26. McKnight, *The Blue Parakeet*, 240, emphasis in original.

27. Derek Tidball and Dianne Tidball, *The Message of Women: Creation, Grace and Gender* (Downers Grove, IL: InterVarsity Press, 2012), 53.

## Chapter 6

1. The verse divisions we use today originated with Robert Estienne (or Stephanus), who included them in the printing of his Greek New Testament in 1551. The first full Bible to be published with verse and chapter divisions was Estienne's edition of the Latin Vulgate in 1555.

2. F. F. Bruce, "The Epistle to the Galatians: A Commentary on the Greek Text," *The New International Greek Testament Commentary* (Grand Rapids, MI: Eerdmans, 1982), 352-354, Kindle.

3. Liturgy: Daily Prayers: "Who Hast Not Made Me a Gentile. "Boston College Center for Christian-Jewish Learning, www.bc.edu/content/dam/files /research_sites/cjl/texts/cjrelations/resources/sourcebook/shelo_asani_goy.htm#:~: text=CE)%20that%20every%20(Jewish, accessed April 2024, emphasis added.

4. Bruce, "The Epistle to the Galatians, A Commentary on the Greek Text," 357, Kindle.

5. Gordon Fee, "Male and Female in the New Creation: Galatians 3:28," in *Discovering Biblical Equality: Complementarity without Hierarchy*, 2nd ed., Ronald W. Pierce and Rebecca Merrill Groothuis ed. (Leicester, England: InterVarsity Press, 2004), 176-77.

6. Scott Bartchy, "Can You Imagine Paul Telling Priscilla Not to Teach?" *Leaven* 4, no. 2 (2012): 21, https://digitalcommons.pepperdine.edu/cgi/viewcontent.cgi?article=1893&context=leaven.

7. Philip B. Payne, *The Bible vs. Biblical Womanhood: How God's Word Consistently Affirms Gender Equality* (Grand Rapids, MI: Zondervan, 2023), 34.

8. Ronald W. Pierce, Cynthia Long Westfall, and Christa L. McKirland, eds., *Discovering Biblical Equality: Biblical, Theological, Cultural, and Practical Perspectives*, 3rd ed. (Downers Grove, IL: InterVarsity Press, 2021), 77.

9. Pierce, Westfall, and McKirland, *Discovering Biblical Equality*, 82.

10. Lucy Peppiatt, *Rediscovering Scripture's Vision for Women: Fresh Perspectives on Disputed Texts* (Downers Grove, IL: InterVarsity Press, 2019), 124.

11. Peppiatt, *Rediscovering Scripture's Vision for Women*, 126.

12. Peppiatt, 126.

13. There are several other verses where this word is used in conjunction with leadership: "If it is to lead, do it diligently" (Rom. 12:8) and "Respect those who ... are over you in the Lord" (1 Thess. 5:12 RSV). Also see 1 Timothy 3:4; 5:17 CEV.

14. Cynthia Long Westfall, *Paul and Gender: Reclaiming the Apostle's Vision for Men and Women in Christ* (Grand Rapids, MI: Baker Academic, 2016), 274.

15. Catherine Clark Kroeger, trans., "John Chrysostom's First Homily on the Greeting to Priscilla and Aquila," *Priscilla Papers* 5, no. 3 (Summer 1991): 18.

16. Peppiatt, *Rediscovering Scripture's Vision for Women*, 128.

17. J. D. G. Dunn, *Romans 9–16*, *Word Biblical Commentary*, vol. 38B (Dallas: Word Books, 1988), 886–90. Dunn observes that the assumption since the twelfth century that Junia was the name of a male, since the person was designated an apostle, is a striking indictment of male presumption regarding the character and structure of earliest Christianity.

18. Quoted in Scot McKnight, *The Blue Parakeet: Rethinking How You Read the Bible*, 2nd ed. (Grand Rapids, MI: Zondervan, 2018), 231.

19. Scot McKnight, *Junia Is Not Alone: Breaking Our Silence about Women in the Bible and the Church Today* (Englewood, CO: Patheos, 2011), 92.

20. Carolyn Osiek and Margaret Y. MacDonald, *A Woman's Place: House Churches in Earliest Christianity*, with Janet H. Tulloch (Minneapolis: Fortress, 2006), 3225.

21. Dorothy A. Lee, *The Ministry of Women in the New Testament: Reclaiming the Biblical Vision for Church Leadership* (Grand Rapids, MI: Baker, 2021), chap. 3, Kindle.

22. Kevin Giles, *Patterns of Ministry among the First Christians*, rev. ed. (Eugene, OR: Cascade Books, 2017), chap 6, Kindle.

23. Amos Yong, *The Spirit Poured Out on All Flesh: Pentecostalism and the Possibility of Global Theology* (Grand Rapids, MI: Baker Academic, 2005), 193.

24. Euodia and Syntyche (Phil. 4:2–3); Nympha (Col. 4:15); Tabitha (Acts 9:36–42); Rufus's mother, Julia (Rom. 13); the sister of Nereus (Rom. 15); Chloe (1 Cor. 1:11); Claudia (2 Tim. 4:21); Apphia (Philem. 1:2); Mary, the mother of John Mark (Acts 12:12); the elect lady (2 John 1:1 ESV); and the women encouraged to prophesy (1 Cor. 11:2–16).

25. Lynn Cohick and Amy Brown Hughes, *Christian Women in the Patristic World: Their Influence, Authority, and Legacy in the Second through Fifth Centuries* (Grand Rapids, MI: Baker Academic, 2017), 19, Kindle.

26. Cohick and Hughes, *Christian Women in the Patristic World*, 19, Kindle.

27. Cohick and Hughes, 86, Kindle.

28. Cohick and Hughes, 19, Kindle.

29. Cohick and Hughes, 21, Kindle.

30. Cohick and Hughes, 275, Kindle.

## Chapter 7

1. Visit www.A21.org for details on what they do and how to get involved.

2. "Why Women Should Be Church Leaders and Preachers // Ask NT Wright Anything," September 25, 2019, Premier On Demand, YouTube video, www.youtube.com/watch?v=os8M9ln2cM0.

3. Lucy Peppiatt, *Rediscovering Scripture's Vision for Women: Fresh Perspectives on Disputed Texts* (Downers Grove, IL: InterVarsity Press, 2019), 155.

4. Eliza Stiles, "Paul's Concern for Ephesus: A Survey of 1 Timothy 2:8–15," *Priscilla Papers* 36, no. 4 (Autumn 2022): 18–22, www.cbeinternational.org/resource/pauls-concern-for-ephesus-a-survey-of-1-timothy-28-15.

5. Peppiatt, *Rediscovering Scripture's Vision for Women*, 146.

6. Sandra L. Glahn, "The Identity of Artemis in First-Century Ephesus," *Bibliotheca Sacra* 172 (July–September 2015): 316–34; Sandra L. Glahn, "The First-Century Ephesian Artemis: Ramifications of Her Identity," *Bibliotheca Sacra* 172 (October–December 2015): 45–69.

7. Gary G. Hoag, *Wealth in Ancient Ephesus and the First Letter to Timothy: Fresh Insights from Ephesiaca* by Xenophon of Ephesus (Winona Lake, IN: Eisenbrauns, 2015).

8. Scot McKnight, "Wealth and the Earliest Christians—Review of Gary Hoag by Lucy Peppiatt," *Jesus Creed* (blog), January 19, 2016, www.patheos.com/blogs /jesuscreed/2016/01/19/wealth-and-the-earliest-christians-a-review-of-gary-hoag -by-lucy-peppiatt.

9. Richard Kroeger and Catherine Clark Kroeger, "1 Timothy 2:9–10 Revisited," *Priscilla Papers* 8, no. 1 (Winter 1994): 4.

10. Hoag, *Wealth in Ancient Ephesus*, 79.

11. Gail Wallace, "Diffusing the 1 Timothy 2:12 Bomb," *The Junia Project Blog*, January 15, 2014, https://juniaproject.com/defusing-1-timothy-212-bomb.

12. Scot McKnight, "What to Say?" *Jesus Creed* (blog), February 23, 2019, www.patheos.com/blogs/jesuscreed/2019/02/27/what-to-say.

13. Philip B. Payne, *The Bible vs. Biblical Womanhood: How God's Word Consistently Affirms Gender Equality* (Grand Rapids, MI: Zondervan, 2023), 155–56.

14. Marg Mowczko, "The Anonymous Man and Woman in 1 Timothy 2:11–15," *Marg Mowczko* (blog), February 4, 2017, https://margmowczko.com/anonymous -man-woman-1-timothy-2.

15. Ronald W. Pierce, Cynthia Long Westfall, and Christa L. McKirland, eds., *Discovering Biblical Equality: Biblical, Theological, Cultural, and Practical Perspectives*, 3rd ed. (Downers Grove, IL: InterVarsity Press, 2021), 477n. The Greek is the gender-inclusive *anthrōpois* and more accurately translated "persons."

16. Peppiatt, *Rediscovering Scripture's Vision for Women*, 151–53.

17. Pierce, Westfall, and McKirland, *Discovering Biblical Equality*, 208.

18. Gail Wallace, "'But What about 1 Timothy 2:12' Ten Talking Points," *The Junia Project*, April 25, 2014, https://juniaproject.com/1-timothy-212-ten-talking-points/.

19. Marg Mowczko, "6 Reasons 1 Timothy 2:12 Is Not as Clear as it Seems," August 3, 2016, https://margmowczko.com/1-timothy-212-not-as-clear/.

20. Johannes P. Louw and Eugene Albert Nida, *Greek-English Lexicon of the New Testament: Based on Semantic Domains* (New York: United Bible Societies, 1996), §37.21.

21. Timothy Friberg, Barbara Friberg, and Neva F. Miller, *Analytical Lexicon of the New Testament* (Grand Rapids, MI: Baker, 2000).

22. Wallace, "Diffusing the 1 Timothy 2:12 Bomb."

23. Martin B. Copenhaver, *Jesus Is the Question: The 307 Questions Jesus Asked and the 3 He Answered* (Nashville: Abingdon Press, 2014), Kindle.

24. Cynthia Long Westfall, *Paul and Gender: Reclaiming the Apostle's Vision for Men and Women in Christ* (Grand Rapids, MI: Baker Academic, 2016), 232, 223.

25. Payne, *The Bible vs. Biblical Womanhood*, 43.

26. Aída Besançon Spencer, *Beyond the Curse: Women Called to Ministry* (Grand Rapids, MI: Baker Academic, 1985), 105.

27. Alan Kreider, *The Patient Ferment of the Early Church: The Improbable Rise of Christianity in the Roman Empire* (Grand Rapids, MI: Baker Academic, 2016), 84.

28. Craig Keener, *Paul, Women and Wives: Marriage and Women's Ministry in the Letters of Paul* (Peabody, MA: 1992), chap. 2, Kindle.

29. Keener, *Paul, Women and Wives*, chap. 3, Kindle, emphasis in original.

30. Scot McKnight, *The Blue Parakeet: Rethinking How You Read the Bible*, 2nd ed. (Grand Rapids, MI: Zondervan, 2018), 261.

## Chapter 8

1. Gillian Zoe Segal, *Getting There: A Book of Mentors (*New York: Abrams Image, 2015), 44–45.

2. Segal, *Getting There*, 45.

3. Abraham Verghese, *Cutting for Stone* (New York: Vintage Books, 2009), 7.

## Chapter 9

1. Quoted in Kate Murphy, *You're Not Listening: What You're Missing and Why It Matters* (New York: Macmillan, 2019), 121.

2. Murphy, *You're Not Listening*, 163.

3. Murphy, 47–60.

4. *Friends*, season 5, episode 16, "The One with the Cop," aired February 25, 1999, on NBC.

5. Murphy, 156.

6. Murphy, 157.

7. Office of the Surgeon General, *Our Epidemic of Loneliness and Isolation 2023: The U.S. Surgeon General's Advisory on the Healing Effects of Social Connection and Community* (Washington, DC: US Department of Health and Human Services, 2023), www.hhs.gov/sites/default/files/surgeon-general-social-connection -advisory.pdf.

8. Murphy, 24.

9. Henri J. M. Nouwen, "March 11: Listening as Spiritual Hospitality," in *Bread for the Journey: A Daybook of Wisdom and Faith* (San Francisco: HarperOne, 2006).

10. Quoted in Ralph G. Martin, *Jennie: The Life of Lady Randolph Churchill* (New York: Signet, 1968), 107, emphasis in original.

11. Martin B. Copenhaver, *Jesus Is the Question: The 307 Questions Jesus Asked and the 3 He Answered* (Nashville: United Methodist Publishing House, 2014), chap. 9, Kindle.

12. Warren Berger, *A More Beautiful Question: The Power of Inquiry to Spark Break-through Ideas* (New York: Bloomsbury, 2014), chap. 2, Kindle.

13. Berger, *A More Beautiful Question*, chap. 2, Kindle.

14. Norman Doidge, *The Brain That Changes Itself: Stories of Personal Triumph from the Frontiers of Brain Science* (New York: Penguin House, 2007), chap. 3, Kindle.

15. Celeste Kidd and Benjamin Y. Hayden, "The Psychology and Neuroscience of Curiosity," National Library of Medicine, November 4, 2015, www.ncbi.nlm.nih .gov/pmc/articles/PMC4635443/.

16. John Dear, *The Questions of Jesus: Challenging Ourselves to Discover Life's Great Answers* (New York: Crown, 2007), Foreword, Kindle.

17. John Hagel III, "Good Leadership Is about Asking Good Questions," *Harvard Business Review*, January 8, 2021, https://hbr.org/2021/01/good-leadership-is -about-asking-good-questions.

## Chapter 10

1. Peter Scazzero, *The Emotionally Healthy Leader: How Transforming Your Inner Life Will Deeply Transform Your Church, Team, and the World* (Grand Rapids, MI: Zondervan, 2015), 55.

2. Adam Grant, "There's a Name for the Blah You're Feeling: It's Called Languishing," *New York Times*, April 19, 2021, www.nytimes.com/2021/04/19/well/mind/covid-mental-health-languishing.html.

3. Scazzero, *The Emotionally Healthy Leader*, 25.

4. Anita Phillips, *The Garden Within: Where the War with Your Emotions Ends and Your Most Powerful Life Begins* (Nashville: Nelson Books, 2023), 79–80, emphasis in original.

5. Phillips, *The Garden Within*, 27.

6. Phillips, 26.

## Chapter 11

1. Napoleon Hill, *Think and Grow Rich* (New York: Barnes and Noble, 2008), 4–5.

2. Ryan Holiday, *The Obstacle Is the Way: The Timeless Art of Turning Trials into Triumph* (New York: Portfolio, 2014), 6–7.

3. Angela Duckworth, *Grit: The Power of Passion and Perseverance* (New York: Scribner, 2016), chap. 3, Kindle.

4. Duckworth, *Grit*, chap. 3, Kindle.

5. Jamie Kern Lima, Instagram post, November 18, 2023, www.instagram.com/jamiekernlima/reel/CzyuAODOefS.

6. The Van Gogh Gallery, "Frequently Asked Questions," accessed December 11, 2023, www.vangoghgallery.com/misc/faq.aspx#.

7. Adam Grant, *Hidden Potential: The Science of Achieving Greater Things* (New York: Viking, 2023), 6.

8. Eugene Peterson, *A Long Obedience in the Same Direction: Discipleship in an Instant Society*, 2nd ed. (Downers Grove, IL: InterVarsity Press, 2000), 17, emphasis added.

9. Peterson, *A Long Obedience*, 17, emphasis added.

10. Malcolm Gladwell, *Outliers: The Story of Success* (Little Brown and Company, Boston, 2008).

11. Ann Voskamp, *One Thousand Gifts: A Dare to Live Fully Right Where You Are* (Grand Rapids, MI: Zondervan), 35.

# Bible Credits

# estherpress

*Our journey invites us deeper into God's Word, where wisdom waits to renew our minds and where the Holy Spirit meets us in discernment that empowers bold action for such a time as this.*

*If we have the courage to say yes to our calling and no to everything else, will the world be ready?*

## JOIN US IN COURAGEOUS LIVING

Your Esther Press purchase helps to equip, encourage, and disciple women around the globe with practical assistance and spiritual mentoring to help them become strong leaders and faithful followers of Jesus.

An imprint of

## DAVID C COOK

*transforming lives together*